COLLABORATIVE RESEARCH
IN MANAGEMENT

COLLABORATIVE RESEARCH IN MANAGEMENT

INSIDE OUT

AMIRAM PORATH

Business books from SAGE
Los Angeles ▪ London ▪ New Delhi ▪ Singapore ▪ Washington DC
www.sagepublications.com

Copyright © Amiram Porath, 2010

All rights reserved. No part of this book may be reproduced or utilized in any form or by any means, electronic or mechanical, including photocopying, recording or by any information storage or retrieval system, without permission in writing from the publisher.

First published in 2010 by

Response Books
Business books from SAGE
B1/I-1 Mohan Cooperative Industrial Area
Mathura Road, New Delhi 110 044, India

SAGE Publications Inc
2455 Teller Road
Thousand Oaks, California 91320, USA

SAGE Publications Ltd
1 Oliver's Yard, 55 City Road
London EC1Y 1SP, United Kingdom

SAGE Publications Asia-Pacific Pte Ltd
33 Pekin Street
#02-01 Far East Square
Singapore 048763

Published by Vivek Mehra for SAGE Publications India Pvt Ltd, typeset in 11/13 pt Berkely Oldstyle Book by Tantla Composition Service Pvt. Ltd., Chandigarh and printed at Chaman Enterprises, New Delhi.

Library of Congress Cataloging-in-Publication Data
Porath, Amiram.
 Collaborative research in management : inside out / Amiram Porath.
  p. cm.
 Includes bibliographical references.
 1. Management—Research. 2. Management—Research—India. I. Title.
HD30.4.P67   658.5'7—dc22   2010   2010033659

ISBN: 978-81-321-0523-7 (PB)

The SAGE Team: Qudsiya Ahmed, Sonalika Rellan, Anju Saxena and Deepti Saxena

Knowledge is the basis for enlightenment to those that light my life—my parents, my children, and my wife.

Contents

List of Figures   xiii
List of Tables   xiv
List of Boxes   xv
List of Abbreviations   xvii
Preface   xix
Acknowledgements   xxi

Part I: Theoretical and Empirical Background

Chapter 1 – Introduction to Collaborative Research   3

- *The Co-opetitor Model*
- *The Environment*
  - *The Players*
  - *Inter-relations*
- *The Conflict Elucidation*
- *Summary*

Chapter 2 – The Challenges Facing Research since WW II: General Overview   14

- *Why have the Costs Increased?*
  - *Development Cycle*
  - *Multi-disciplinary Sectors*
- *Are there Industries which are More Prone to Ever Increasing R&D Costs?*
- *Where does the Financing come from?*
- *What Alternatives do the Firms use to Reduce the Load?*

- Pass the Costs to the Customers or Marketing Chains
- Subsidize the Cost from External Sources
- Absorb the Costs and Reduce Profits
- Basic Terms
  - Terms and Definitions
- Summary

Chapter 3 – Forms of Collaborative Research   27

- The Triple Helix
- The Place of R&D and CR in Firm Activity
- R&D Collaboration Forms
- Solitary R&D
- RJV (Research Joint Venture)
- R&D Consortium
- Cross Licensing Agreement (CLA)
- Other Forms of Industry–Academy Cooperation
  - Licensing
  - Contracted Research
- Advantages and Disadvantages of Different Collaboration Forms
- Summary
- Appendix

Chapter 4 – The Multi-dimensional Model   47

- R&D Definition
  - Research
  - Development
- Dimensions of the Model
  - Legal
  - Players
- Summary

Chapter 5 – The Partners and their Roles   56

- *The Dual Perspective*
- *Industry*
- *R&D Benefits*
- *Industry Scale of Values*
- *Industry Fears*
  - *Spillovers*
  - *CR Worries*
- *Academy Point of View*
  - *Applied Research*
- *Partner Roles*
  - *The Sequential View*
  - *The Parallel View*
- *Summary*

Part II: Practical Aspects

Chapter 6 – When should You get into a Collaborative Project?   77

- *Formative Process*
  - *General Relevance*
  - *Relevant Empirical Research*
  - *Focused Research*
  - *Broad Research*
  - *Theoretical Background Summary*
- *The Structured Program (SP) Model*
  - *Parameters of the SP Model*
- *Decision Parameter*
  - *Inherent Dangers*
  - *Inherent Potential*
- *Summary*

Chapter 7 – The Decisive Role of Intellectual Property   94

- *Defining IP*
- *IP as a Strategic Asset*
- *Formulating IPR*
- *The Outlook of the Different Partners on IP and IPR*
- *Benefit of IP to the Academy: A Short Philosophical Emphasis*
- *Do's and Don'ts in IPR*
- *Where are the Danger Points? The Don'ts*
- *Who should Decide?*
- *Who should Define IP?*
- *Summary*

Chapter 8 – The Academy–Industry Troubled Cooperation   109

- *The Natural Conflict*
  - *The Academic Culture*
  - *The Industrial Culture*
- *The Cultural Differences Summarized*
- *Summary*

Chapter 9 – Government: The Silent Partner   121

- *The Government Rationale Regarding Support to Collaborative Research*
  - *The Economic Perspective*
  - *The Political Perspective*
- *The Government Dilemma*
- *The WTO Perspective*
  - *Basic Rules*
- *Problems of Governmental Financing Mechanisms*
- *Summary*

Chapter 10 – How to Run a Successful Collaborative Project   135

- *Basic Requirements*
  - *Central Management*
  - *Partner Management*
  - *Interfacing*
- *Who should Manage?*
- *How to Manage?*
- *Summary*

Chapter 11 – How to Avoid the Pitfalls of the Collaborative Project   149

- *The Academic Point of View*
- *The Industrial Point of View*
  - *Strategic Aspects*
  - *Direct Economic Aspects*
  - *Licensing Aspects*
  - *Long-term Capabilities*
- *The Impact of Sector Affiliation*
- *Summary*

Chapter 12 – Left Out: How to Compensate   161

- *The First Stage of the Reaction: An Analysis*
- *Environmental Analysis*
- *How to get the Data without Participating?*
- *Benefits of Standardization*
- *Retiring from the Consortium*
- *Strategy*
- *Types of Factors*
  - *Technological Breakthrough*
  - *Failure of the Technology to Perform*
- *Summary*

Chapter 13 – The Future of Collaborative Research   174

- *Summary*

Chapter 14 – How to Build a Successful Collaborative Research Program   179

- *General*
- *The Rationale*
- *Adapting Existing Programs*
- *The First Step: Analyzing*
- *SWOT*
  - *SWOT Drawing*
- *Designing the Program*
- *Needs and Goals: Definition*
- *Program Examples*
  - *Basic to Applied Research (BAR)*
  - *Validation and Technology Transfer (VATT)*
  - *Non-generic Cooperation (NGC)*
- *Summary*

Chapter 15 – National Application (India)   192

- *India: A Country Sample*
- *India: Academic Research Infrastructure*
  - *General*
  - *Basic Parameters*
- *India: Scientific Excellence*
- *Research and Education System*
- *India: Research Investment*
- *India: Industry–Academy Cooperation*
- *India: Future Development Possibilities*
- *Summary*

Bibliography   206
About the Author   211

List of Figures

3.1	R&D Interaction with Firm Function	29
3.2	Role of Generic R&D	29
3A.1	The Israeli Magnet Approval Process	46
5.1	Government–Industry Interaction	57
5.2	Government–Academy Interaction	57
5.3	The Spillover Conflict	65
5.4	Sequential View	70
5.5	Parallel View	73
6.1	DOR Model	85
6.2	The Structured Program (SP) Model	87
8.1	Independent Evaluation vs. Reduced Personnel	114
9.1	Basic vs. Applied Research	124
9.2	Authority Influence from Consortium to SRJV	126
13.1	Increased CR	177
14.1	Competence Centers Genealogical Map	181
15.1	Central Government Departments Dealing with Research	199

List of Tables

3.1	Free RJV vs. SRJV Summary	36
4.1	Legal Parameters of the Model	50
4.2	Players' (Government) Parameters	51
4.3	Players' (Academy) Parameters	53
4.4	Players' (Industry) Parameters	54
9.1	Benefit and Dangers in Supporting SRJV	133
11.1	Licensing Parameters	157

List of Boxes

1.1	Academic Partner Specification	12
1.2	Industrial Partner Specification	12
2.1	Engineering Economics	15
2.2	The IMEC Case	17
2.3	Nano Sector Entry Cost	17
2.4	R&D Financing Sources	20
2.5	Role of the R&D Service Provider	21
3.1	Solitary R&D	31
3.2	The Free RJV—the US Model	33
3.3	The Structured RJV	33
3.4	Magnet Program–SRJV	35
3.5	Mechanics Consortium	38
3.6	CLA	39
3.7	Low-tech Example	43
3.8	Long-term Research	43
5.1	Product Cost Reduction	58
5.2	Next Generation R&D	59
5.3	Spillover	64
5.4	IP Limitations	64
5.5	Academic Performance Evaluation	67
5.6	Magnet 2	71
6.1	Insiders and Left Out's	91
7.1	Academy–Industry IP Agreement	95
7.2	IPR	97

7.3	IPR– Different Partners	100
7.4	IP–Revenues	103
7.5	IP–Publications	105
7.6	IP–Publications 2	105
7.7	IP–FP 6	106
7.8	IP–Joint Ownership	107
8.1	Academic Warranty	115
8.2	Academic Declaration	116
8.3	Impressive Discoveries	118
9.1	Eureka	126
9.2	Possible SRJV–Government	128
9.3	Possible SRJV–Government 2	128
9.4	SRJV Finance–Magnet Program	132
10.1	Overcoming Financial Management Problems	136
10.2	SRJV Finance–Complications	139
10.3	SRJV Finance–Complications 2	140
10.4	SRJV–Scientific Management	141
10.5	SRJV–Administrative Management	142
10.6	SRJV–Management Demands	144
11.1	SRJV–Management Difficulties	151
11.2	SRJV–IP Management	155
11.3	SRJV–Liability	156
11.4	SRJV–Knowledge Transfer	158
12.1	Spillover Legend	171
13.1	SRJV–Repeatability of Participation	177
14.1	VC Market	180
14.2	Regionalism	182
14.3	BAR	187
14.4	VATT	190
14.5	NGC	191

List of Abbreviations

BAR	Basic to Applied Research
CLA	Cross Licensing Agreement
CR	Collaborative Research
CSIR	Council of Scientific and Industrial Research
DAE	Department of Atomic Energy
DBT	Department of Biotechnology
DOD	Department of Ocean Development
DoS	Department of Space
DSIR	Department of Scientific and Industrial Research
DST	Department of Science and Technology
ER	Electronic Region
EU	European Union
EUFP	EU Framework Programs
FDA	Food and Drug Administration
FET	Future Emerging Technology
IC	Intellectual Capital
ICT	Information and Communication Technologies
IP	Intellectual Property
IPR	Intellectual Property Rights
MR	Mechanical Region
NEST	Newly Emerging Science & Technology
NGC	Non-Generic Cooperation
R&D	Research and Development
RJV	Research Joint Venture
SEM	Scanning Electron Microscope
SMEs	Small Medium Enterprises
SP	Structured Program
SRJV	Structured Research Joint Venture

SSA	Specific Support Action
STPI	Software Technology Parks of India
SWOT	Strengths, Weaknesses, Opportunities, Threats
TEM	Transmission Electron Microscopy
TT	Technology Transfer
TTC	Technology Transfer Company
TTO	Technology Transfer Office
VATT	Validation and Technology Transfer

Preface

PURPOSE OF THE BOOK

This book describes Collaborative Research (CR) with a dual purpose. Theoreticians and researchers of organizational forms will find a description of the organization of CR from different points of view and covering different species of CR.

For practitioners, either as potential participants or as decision makers, charged with forming frameworks for CR, this book will offer insights and better understanding of the point of view of the other players.

Other books have discussed CR trying to determine if it is good or bad, what should be done, and so on. In this book, the outlook is more of an operational model for decision makers. If you wish to increase the cooperation between academy and industry you should take certain actions, and if you wish to create an industrial critical mass, you should structure the program differently. For industrial managers and academia leaders, the book will describe the effect of the structure on the output so as to allow adaptation of expectations.

STRUCTURE OF THE BOOK

The book is divided into two parts. The first being an introduction to the topic of CR, describes the reasons behind it, its theoretical background, the role of the partners involved, and their interaction. This part is intended for students and researchers interested in studying the field of CR.

The second part is practical advice to practitioners from the academic administration, industrial managers, government and regional government officials, and their consultants.

Acknowledgements

This book has been a single person's work supported by many. The scientific parts which are also related to my PhD thesis were guided and helped by my guides Prof. Tzvi Raz (RIP) and Prof. Eli Segev. The book would have never been published without the guidance and advice from Prof. Shlomo Maital and the wonderful people at SAGE Publications.

It is my family that I would like to thank most of all, my parents who have given me the guidance and the outlook on life to allow me to write the book; my children Ariel, Yael, and Ayala, who paid most dearly by giving me the time to write; and most of all my wife Marcia Neomy, who helped me find the balance in my life and in all my endeavors.

Part I

Theoretical and Empirical Background

Introduction to Collaborative Research

This chapter introduces Collaborative Research (CR) as a concept, and the relevant parameters influencing it. The basic need for CR is defined below and is accompanied by some of the relevant research. The purpose of this chapter is to allow the reader to familiarize himself with the concept of CR, and to allow the creation of a joint platform for the discussion of concepts. In aid of this purpose, the chapter introduces the basic definitions to be used through this book, and the basic outlying concept.

Collaborative Research is defined for our purposes,[1] *as research jointly executed by at least two different entities one from a profit-oriented sector, and another from a non-profit oriented sector.* The definition of collaboration requires that at least two entities, entirely different from each other cooperate.[2] The problematic, more lifelike and, therefore, more analysis-worthy research is the cooperation between non-equal partners with different purposes. The requirement for different entities with the profit and non-profit characteristics leads to their conflict. Industries collaborating with each other are so very similar; they lack the cultural abyss that exists between the academic world and the industry. The lack of

---

[1] Working definitions will be marked in *italic*, while definitions borrowed from other sources will be presented in quotations.

[2] For the purposes of this book, the cooperation between a research entity and production entity of the same corporation is not considered as Collaborative Research.

the cultural abyss is especially evident when one considers vertical and horizontal integration. The firms in sectors where such integration happens would be deemed identical from the point of view of their research. The same applies to two entities from the non-profit sector. Only cross-sector cooperation can be defined as a collaboration of significantly different entities.

The ever-shortening product life cycle, and the technological revolutions are placing increasingly heavy demands on the development departments of the industry, resulting in making the technological world more competitive. These trends make the technological sectors in the industry more open to cooperation (Kaiser, 2002b). In some highly competitive sectors, a single firm cannot sustain the competitive advantage for very long without heavy investment in R&D. Such heavy investment taxes the annual turnover of the firms and attempts are always made to reduce it. One of the simplest ways is to share the burden of R&D between firms. The main problem in R&D cooperation between firms is that, if the firms are technologically close enough to cooperate, they are probably also close enough to be competitors in at least one of the following ways:

1. Market competition: similar or close products competing in the market.
2. Resource competition
    a. Production resources.
    b. Technology resources (including technological man power and access to knowledge).
    c. Marketing resources.
3. Strategic partnerships

In their definition of Co-Opetitors (Brown and Eisenhardt, 1998), they described the interesting enemy–friend relationships that complicate the commercial scenery. This is an extremely important aspect. The Co-Opetitor syndrome cannot be neglected if assumed as a basic assumption that the analysis is of partners from the same sector. At every CR project comprising more than two partners, at least two will come from the same sector,[3] either academy or industry. Among the same sector partners, the Co-Opetitor issues are very strong. The firms trying to collaborate under that atmosphere of potential competition have to lay down the strictest set of rules of cooperation so as to avoid conflict.

THE CO-OPETITOR MODEL

In 1984, a change occurred in the EU with the announcement of the first Framework Program allowing cooperation in generic R&D between research organizations and firms competing in the same markets (EU, 2003; 2006). Up to that point, the authorities were worried that such cooperation will lead firms to collusion in the market place. It was in that year, that for the first time US authorities allowed firms to cooperate in R&D consortia, while making sure the participants remained competitors in the market place. The Research Joint Venture (RJV) and the Structured Research Joint Venture (SRJV) did not appear out of the blue. Since the 1950s, independent R&D has met with increasing difficulties regarding costs, and especially set-up costs (Kaiser, 2002b). The most obvious way to overcome this problem is to divide the cost and reduce it to a single player. One way to do this is through the formation of an R&D consortium, *a group of research entities that come together to carry out a specific research project (defined by the character of the research—basic, generic, applied or other; and scope of research), for a predefined time frame (either by calendar or achievement)*. However, this idea has its own problems: ownership and distribution of resulting knowledge, and collusion in the market, to name a few. The US anti-trust laws forbade R&D consortia in the US until the enactment of the National Cooperation Research Act, 1984. This Act allowed the formation of such consortia and required their registration. A similar change

---

[3]Sector refers here to industry or academy, not to different industrial sectors.

occurred in the EU, in 1985 (Miyagiwa and Ohno, 2002). These amendments resulted in governments actively supporting the formation of R&D consortia, mainly by sponsoring programs (such as the Framework Programs), and promoting their activities in selected technologies (Laredo, 1998). The original reason for prohibiting the formation of such consortia was the fear that their activities could lead to cartelization in the product markets as well. While the contribution of sponsored R&D aimed at the development of products is clear and understandable, the value of the above-mentioned national programs in areas not requiring large capital investment in R&D (for example, software) is not so obvious (Luukkonen, 1998). In his 1990 article, Rosenberg analyzes the reasons behind the involvement of firms in basic research. He presents the interest behind the firm's involvement in basic research, based on economic and economically linked parameters, such as first-movers' advantages, long-term payoffs, possibility to capitalize a return on investment in spite of spillovers, and as a leading route to applied research. An additional argument presented, is the link to the academy and research organizations, but not from the RJV point of view. The article mentions some specific cases but presents no empirical data.

The US NSF[4] defined the different types of R&D activities as follows (as appears in the NSF website):

> Basic Research is the pursuit of new scientific knowledge or understanding that does not have specific immediate commercial objectives, although it may be in fields of present or potential commercial interest.
>
> Applied Research applies the findings of basic research or other existing knowledge toward discovering new scientific knowledge that has specific commercial objectives with respect to new products, services, processes, or methods.
>
> Development is the systematic use of knowledge or understanding gained from research or practical experience directed toward the production or significant improvement of useful products, services, processes, or methods, including the design and development of prototypes, materials, devices and systems.

---

[4]NSF website. (2008). http://www.nsf.gov/statistics/randeff/business.cfm

Generic Research will be used here to describe Applied Research, at the stage of discovering the new knowledge intended to have commercial use, and the translation of the basic knowledge into such applied knowledge. Thereby, Generic Research is on the border line between Applied Research and Basic Research. At this interface, Basic Research results and knowledge are expected to be transferred among organizations dealing with the same, as well as, to organizations dealing with Applied Research, and potentially also with Development. Among their functions, these organizations (in the second group) would be expected to define the commercial usage and potential for the future use of the knowledge, and be able to evaluate or direct the Generic Research towards obtaining the research goals.

This is the current active field of Technology Transfer (TT) between research organizations and industries that has come more and more into focus in the last decade. While TT has many aspects, and can be viewed as a legal action, as a commercial action (a sale, activity in a market, etc.), and in many other forms, the CR analyzed in this book, is a mechanism for transferring knowledge. Most of the views mentioned here deal with one aspect of the transfer that is, mostly with ownership, rights and benefits, and rarely look at the way in which knowledge itself is transferred for further utilization. It is important to remember that Generic Research is far from the commercial benefits of production and sales, further away than Development, and the furthest part of Applied Research. It is a link in the chain, and it is fairly hidden from the public. It is also important to understand at this point that CR and SRJV specifically do not contradict TT methodologies or agreements rather these will accompany the CR or SRJV according to the framework in which they work, and will form an integral part of such activity. In fact, they are required to complete the CR and SRJV picture (see Chapter 7). In order to keep the book as a general handbook for CR interested parties, the finer details of Intellectual Property and Technology Transfer contractual details will not be described here in minutiae. Basics and critical points will be discussed and further reading maybe recommended.

In his research, Porath (2007) presents empirical data showing that firms dealing with Generic Research under SRJV perform better economically during periods of crises, controlling for size and sector. These economic benefits (revenues) cannot be derived directly from the specific SRJV's the performing firms are participating in at that time. Therefore, it does indicate some capability in the firms that links their performance in the market with their involvement in the SRJV. Firms involved in such SRJVs showed involvement in that activity (even if only in a monitoring and approval capacity) of upper management levels. Such involvement contributed without doubt to the better understanding of these management levels of changes and trends in the markets, and probably allowed firms to better prepare for difficulties, and capitalize better on successes. With the advance in understanding of different R&D phases, this specific fear subsided. Economic models have shown the effect of combining improved controls over cartelization, thus reducing the public authority's fear of cartelization, with active encouragement of the formation of the R&D consortia, which leads to a decrease in the apprehension firms may have regarding Collaborative Research and while increases the social benefit ('D'Aspremont and Jacquemin, 1988; Laredo, 1998; Luukkonen, 1998; 1992; Kaiser, 2002a; Kamien et al., 1992; Kamien and Zang, 2000; Miyagiwa and Ohno, 2002), leading to a decrees in the apprehension regarding Collaborative Research. Therefore, as of the 1980s a new form of R&D consortia emerged—RJVs supported by government or regional entities. The US Act of 1984 does not support RJVs financially, but other models such as the EU Framework Programs do. In these cases, RJVs supported by the governmental or regional entities, tend to deal with Generic Research, for the following reasons:

1. It is easier to allay fears of opportunism in Generic Research than in product development. The distance from the market place allowing each firm to develop its own

unique set of products based on the firm's special capabilities and resources decreases the fear.
2. The general nature of the research results enables the governmental entities to promote the programs and facilitate the formation of RJVs.

From the government viewpoint, it is easier to support Generic Research than product development improving competitiveness for a portion of the national/regional industry firms that are members of the RJV. It is easier to explain in terms of spending public funds on improving the economic benefits of specific firms. Improving the competitiveness of a sector is done against the background of external competitiveness. The support of a single specific firm is performed against the background of internal national/regional competition, as opposed to the support of a sector. Real technological advantage is no longer achieved just by development. For real, sustainable technological competitive advantage, the industry requires the cooperation of the academy, in all sectors. The required cooperation is not so trivial; the cooperation between any two separate entities is difficult enough, and even more so when the entities come from different cultural backgrounds, have different aims, and a different set of values. The search to increase understanding of the reasons for forming such consortia—their various forms and unique advantages and disadvantages, optimal management of each form, results and benefits, and the best ways to encourage formation for achieving benefits—are current research areas in several academic disciplines, as well as, a pragmatic interest among policy makers and practitioners.

THE ENVIRONMENT

The best way to understand the phenomenon of Collaborative Research (CR) is to start from the environment in which CR operates and the players involved. We shall begin by identifying and characterizing the players (stakeholders), followed by their interrelations, and ending with their impact on the environment.

The Players

When looking at the R&D environment in developed and developing countries, one finds the following categories of players:

1. National/regional/governmental research centers and institutes
2. Public universities
3. Private research centers
4. Industry

National research center and institutes: Are governmental or government owned research institutes aimed at furthering the national[5] research agenda, and normally have a strong economic rational, as their basis.

Public universities: Both nationally and regionally, owned and financed universities, promoting academic education and training, as well as basic research. Normally, the basic research will be done according to scientific interest.

Private research centers: Are private research institutes, firms or universities, perusing economic and non-economic interests. The research performed, is done according to the economic or non-economic interests of the organization.

Industry is characterized by economic value driven research. The research is aimed at the creation of financial economic gains via products or process (including services). These players do most of the development, engineering and market-driven product creation. The four types of players are not all necessarily present in all national arenas. At least two, the public research universities and the industry, are always present. The other two types depend on the level of development and the size of the economy.

---

[5]National here represents both national and regional.

Inter-relations

In the following chapters, the inter-relations between the two minimum players will be analyzed. At this stage, it is enough to state that the differences in the aims and goals, and therefore in the nature, character, and internal culture of the players are the basis for the research interest and of this book. It is the differences that make the collaboration difficult and fruitful at the same time. Hopefully, understanding will allow it to be fruitful and less difficult.

THE CONFLICT ELUCIDATION

The best way to introduce the interesting facets of the Academy–Industry cooperation would be to present their cooperation through a series of conflicts. The rest of this book will deal with the different conflicts from different points of view and the best ways to handle the conflicts. The development of Collaborative Research, its increased usage, and the fact that it will probably become even more popular, promises great rewards to those able to understand its formation and function mechanisms, and the ability to control the cooperation in order to achieve the requested goals. The EU has recognized this potential for cooperation that would allow reaching new summits of economic growth through the utilization of research capabilities linked to economic ventures and interests (EU, 2006). It has formed the Open Method of Coordination committees to better address it, with regards to, increasing cooperation between such different entities, and allowing them to find their own grounds for cooperation, with the Commission leading them all the way. The governmental role depicted is more of governance and monitoring, and less of leading. The leadership is left for the players in the market–field. When trying to understand the core of the Academy–Industry cooperation problem, one should remember that the conflict better illustrates the difficulties.

Box 1.1: Academic Partner Specification

An industrial firm is looking for an academic partner in order to develop a strategic technology that will assist it in getting crucial marketing advantage. The firm goes to a consultant in order to get some assistance in finding the best partner, and is requested to submit a list of characteristics of the ideal partner. This is a part of the list:

1. An academic partner that is financially independent and can reduce the financial load of research and development;
2. Partner that will maintain confidentiality at normally acceptable levels in the sector;
3. Will form a strategic exclusive partnership with the firm;
4. A partner who will be highly integrated into the relevant market sector; and
5. Should be familiar with the marketing aspects of the sector influencing the further development.

Does that partial description fit any academic partner familiar to you?

Box 1.2: Industrial Partner Specification

A university interested in improving its cooperation with the industry seeks an industrial partner via a partnering website. The university has to place the profile of the ideal partner and here are some of points from that profile: Interested in basic research leading to scientific breakthroughs allowing publishing in leading journals; allowing radical changes in research direction, according to results; allowing free and open discussion regarding results and research direction with other academic and non-academic bodies.

Do you know any firm that would agree to such a basis for a strategic alliance?

The conflict between publishing and confidentiality is clear and well defined, therefore, it can also be solved using contractual means and management systems. The abyss between research management and organizational character of different partners are more difficult to overcome. These are cultural differences, are harder to define, and therefore harder to solve. This issue will be dealt with later in the book.

SUMMARY

The introductory chapter introduced the reader to CR and its environment, and has shown the central role CR is gaining with time. The basic need for CR has been defined. The evolutionary process in which CR has developed in the practical world, and the accompanying research has been briefly presented. Following the explanation of the basic needs contributing to the evolution of CR, the different partners involved have been defined, and their inter-relations been briefly depicted. Examples for the different approaches to CR, as well as, the governmental point of view, have been presented. These will be further discussed in the following chapters.

In order to discuss CR in detail, this chapter presented to its readers the concept of CR to allow the creation of a joint platform of concepts for discussion. For that purpose, the chapter introduced the basic definitions to be used through this book and the basic outlying concept. After presenting the background, it is now possible to progress.

2

The Challenges Facing Research since WW II: General Overview

In the introductory chapter, we have seen that the industry in knowledge-based sectors is required to invest in R&D in order to survive, and to further promote its position. There are industrial sectors where, the short life cycle of the products, the fast advance of technology, and the pressure to reduce costs, results in a situation where R&D expenses run very high (especially in fields when the research is closer to the final product; micro to nano electronics and biotechnology). An additional aspect increasing the R&D burden is the introduction of multi-disciplinary research and aspects. Firms facing the R&D race theoretically have three options, but out of them, only one is optimal (for small as well as large firms) in the long term: subsidizing the R&D cost from external sources. Luckily, such sources exist. However, finance probably does not answer all, and here is where Collaborative Research and the Academy enter. When dealing with R&D cost load, the following questions form the basis for analysis:

1. Why have the costs increased?
2. Are there industries which are more prone to ever increasing R&D costs?
3. Where does the financing come from?
4. What alternatives do the firms use to reduce the load?

WHY HAVE THE COSTS INCREASED?

At the end of the WW II, the technological world having developed huge production facilities, and mastered to a large extent the unification in design and production, had started the fast track of technological advancement. The increasing incorporation of electronics into mechanical products, and the appearance of the communication industries (television and other electronic systems) have started industries where product life cycles are shortening and the development race is intensive. An important index is the Moore Law regarding the rate of development.

Development Cycle

The increased development cycle has created a need for ever-more expensive R&D. The costs of R&D have placed ever-growing strains on the industries involved (Kaiser, 2002b) and forced them to seek ways to reduce the load, without compromising on the results. The reasons for the fast development cycles have also combined with the need to update the knowledge in the firms faster than ever, which has increased the strain on the development units. Moreover, the cost of personnel has increased, and in several cases, that is the major load on the R&D system (software and related sectors).

Box 2.1: Engineering Economics

> During the High-Tech boom in the 1990's, engineering (electrical and software) costs had risen to about 100,000 US$ per year per person. At that time, computer costs had come down to under 1,000 US$ per unit. Thus, the engineering costs were 100 times more than the computer it used for work. If considering the lifetime of the computer and not the purchase price, as the computer was depreciated over three years, the engineer cost 300 times more than the equipment.

Contd. Box 2.1

Contd. Box 2.1

> In Israel, the cost was not just the salary, even if it was slightly less than in the US, but the additional working conditions such as costly lunches and recreation equipment added for the benefit of the workers.
> It was the time for desperately seeking additional workers for projects. A certain international corporation in communication used the migration from the former USSR to Israel to recruit workers still in the former USSR, train them for software design and programming, and bring them to Israel after having them sign the employment contract in the former USSR, with conditions fitting their former environment. But, the conditions were not the problem; the existence of human resources available for hire was the problem.

Multi-disciplinary Sectors

The trends towards multi-disciplinary activities are ever increasing in all sectors. With the advent of nano sciences (nano bio, nano materials), multi-disciplinarity is becoming a necessity as the differences between chemistry, physics, biology, and biotechnology are becoming ever more blurred. The combination of Information and Communication Technologies (ICT) and medicine, and communication, and other related fields is also increasing (bio-informatics and other fields). To cope with the multi-disciplinary demands, the firms need to invest in new and unknown fields for them (software firms with biology, pharmaceuticals firms with information technologies), and that increases the direct R&D load, as well as, increasing the load on the firms' management. For such activities the combination of the R&D efforts by several entities, each specializing in its own field, can reduce the direct R&D costs for sure, but it may, however, have a negative effect on the R&D management costs. Here, the importance of the specific tool for cooperation is very important (see Chapter 3). The increasing need for the new activities to deal with research on the basic level, or close to it, will increase the need for ever more resources, as the scale of activities is becoming greater. The cost increase comprises of the increasing need for more expansive equipment, and the need for newly trained human resources, which will be scarce and therefore costly in the short term, until the education and training systems take on the new load.

Box 2.2: The IMEC Case

An interesting case to view in this aspect is that of IMEC in Flanders, Belgium. Founded in 1984, IMEC deals with applied research in the IC field with the mission: "To perform R&D, **ahead of industrial needs by 3 to 10 years**, in microelectronics, nanotechnology, design methods and technologies for ICT systems" (IMEC Website, 2008). With more than 1,300 employees' collaborations and more than 500 partners worldwide, and over 20 spin-offs, IMEC is working through collaboration with different partners in the field between the academy and the industry, with a clear agenda for the industry. As stated in the IMEC website: "In 2005, IMEC's revenues rose by 29.6% to 162 million euro. Today, IMEC thereby generates 82% of its total budget (197 million euro), the remaining 18% being funded by the Flemish community."

IMEC is an example to the vast amounts that need to be generated to promote R&D in areas like IC. It is also a "Best Practice" for cooperation between research organizations and industry, and the beneficial impact of such activities on the economy.

When looking at a single firm, trying to enter a knowledge-based sector or maintain its position in such a sector, it is important to understand the effort it puts into R&D activities, and the financial burden an R&D infrastructure can have on it.

Box 2.3: Nano Sector Entry Cost

The entry of a firm in the sensors market into nanotechnology has been costly. The need to acquire abilities in TEM and SEM technologies has been the major cost incurred, and the equipment has been a significant part of it. However, the need to acquire at the same time, the personnel specializing in the relevant technologies, has been another very significant part of the cost. Here, although a lot of academic work has been done the firms still need to purchase the equipment and develop the capabilities to acquire the technologies developed in the industry (Kamien et al., 1992). An investment of 3 million US$ went into the purchase of the equipment. However, the cost of the four people required for working it for three years[6] at a monthly cost of 8,000 US$ was 1,152,000 US$.

---

[6]Time required to attain expert level.

Through the example given in Box 2.3, it is important to understand some characteristics of the sector. In a less knowledge-intensive sector, the equipment for production or research is depreciated by use. However, with the fast turn-around of technologies, features required and the constant pressure to reduce costs this sector behaves otherwise. The equipment is depreciated in that area not by usage, but by technology advance. The personnel at the same time require further training on a continuous basis and this increases the costs. The personnel is costly from the beginning as it requires people trained from the outset (technicians, engineers, and research personnel MSc and PhD); and further training to keep up with development, increases their costs. The sector relevance of the R&D cost is discussed in the following section.

ARE THERE INDUSTRIES WHICH ARE MORE PRONE TO EVER INCREASING R&D COSTS?

When industries suffer from high-technology intensity in the products, where the main drive for competition in the market is the features of the products, we see several characteristics resulting from the type of market.

High-Tech market characteristics:

1. Short product life cycle
2. Product prices reduce with advance in product life
3. Product sales derived by performance and not price
4. Product is grouped by generation

As the competition increases and there is a need to produce more and more products with increased technological performance, the new products are stretching the limits of the knowledge and technology in the field. The firms are driven towards the cutting edge of technology, and are slowly invading the realm of the applied and later, basic research. However, basic research is much riskier than development; the chances for failure are higher. The increased risk requires (do not forget the pressure to come up with new products on time) the firms to manage several projects at the same time, and to try and incorporate other disciplines where the potential is not yet exhausted. That combination of several parallel projects, multi-disciplinarity, and basic research increases the costs of the R&D activities. So, in sectors where the product life cycle is getting ever shorter (a symptom), the R&D costs are liable to increase in a positive feedback loop cycle. Thus, we would expect the electronics, communications, medical equipment, and pharmaceuticals to see the R&D costs increase. This permanent increase poses a serious problem to the firms, as presented in the following section.

WHERE DOES THE FINANCING COME FROM?

As stated by the articles of Luukkonen (1998, 2000), the main purpose of multi national research support programs is to reduce the risk inherent in research. A similar task can be attributed, also to regional or governmental agencies supporting R&D actions intended to increase the economic competitive advantage of the firms in their domains, especially when dealing with Generic Research. The firms faced with increasing R&D costs face a strategic problem. Due to the R&D costs, which reduce its profitability, the overall the performance of the firm, is diminished. Tax incentives to perform R&D are part of a solution—potential solutions—but are not remedying the problem. The scope of solutions, potentially available to firms, is presented in Box 2.4. When the R&D costs increase, the firms at least enjoy the knowledge that the main driving factors for sales are the features and performance of the products, and they are less sensitive to the price. That allows the firms to collect high prices for the new generation of products. Some of the additional R&D costs are transferred to the clients, but some are eating into the profits of the firms. The firms in these markets face the market cannibalization conflict.

Box 2.4: R&D Financing Sources

A firm has a new product—that has cost a huge part of last year's revenue—about to be launched into the market. The market is currently dominated by the firm's last year prize product that has become a milk cow, generating the generous revenues, allowing the firm to develop the new prize income. Launching the product into the market will eat not only into the revenues of the competitors but also into the revenues of the firm replacing its milk cow product. This replacement will not allow the firm to recover the development costs of the old product. To eat or not to eat—that is the question. The reason the firm had to develop the new product, and the reason behind finally launching it into the market, is the fact that the competitors are also developing new products, and the market does not forgive a firm lagging behind with new technology products. The firm has to judge correctly the moment to launch the new product, in order to be ahead of the competition, and retain the market share and the income, but late enough to milk the maximum from the old product already in the market.

So, the firms raise finance from sales, from continually raising funds from the public, and from acquiring assets allowing additional revenues. The increased costs are hurting the firms and they are seeking ways to reduce the costs.

One of the reasons behind the delay in the entrance of the third-generation of communication technology was the reluctance of the firms to cannibalize their second-generation products.

WHAT ALTERNATIVES DO THE FIRMS USE TO REDUCE THE LOAD?

When firms are faced with costs they can do three things:

1. Pass the costs to the customers or marketing chains
2. Subsidize the cost from external sources
3. Absorb the costs and reduce the profits

Pass the Costs to the Customers or Marketing Chains

This is by far the easiest decision for the firm, when the market allows it. However, in most technological sectors, the trend is reducing costs, and therefore, this solution is not viable as a permanent method. From a strategic point of view, such a step would open the firm to a pricing attack by the competition in the market, and is therefore, not recommended. In sectors where there is a strong pressure to reduce costs, a firm raising prices to cover R&D expenses would play directly to the hands of the competition. Most firms, therefore, would have to select one of the other solutions. In most markets in order to use this solution, the firms would have to capitalize on early sales at high prices, which would position their products at the high end. Firms specializing in that sort of market positioning, open themselves to risks of global slow down or market shifts, more than other firms do. In any case, this would not be a solution open to firms in sectors basing their income on mass sales.

Subsidize the Cost from External Sources

As mentioned in the previous section, one alternative to raise the funds is trying to pass the costs to the customers or marketing chains. What other alternatives do the firms have?

One of the major costs in R&D is the cost of the infrastructure. To avoid that cost, the firm can purchase the knowledge. Purchasing the knowledge itself would reduce some of the basic investment in infrastructure, and some of the work invested. However, it is important to remember that the closer to the product the knowledge is, the higher the price. The price of the knowledge is comprised partly from the risk already over come, and the risk remaining before reaching the market.

Box 2.5: Role of the R&D Service Provider

> A start-up required a model of the product in order to raise the next round of the investment. However, in order to produce the model, a manufacturing infrastructure was required. However, the investment in the equipment, not considering the investment in acquiring the expertise of the personnel to make it well, was higher than the expected raised capital. The start-up was obliged to purchase R&D services from a research

Contd. Box 2.5

Contd. Box 2.5

> organization owning the infrastructure and produce a model that helped it raise the required capital.
> At a later stage the firm wanted to start its own manufacturing infrastructure. It used the services of the research organization, in order to try different types of equipment, and decide on the equipment most suitable for their future production line. This saved the start-up a huge investment in potentially risky infrastructure.

For firms purchasing the knowledge, the main saving is by reducing the risk involved in a research, that is, close to the technological edge of the knowledge. However, there is still risk, and especially for firms in the knowledge-based sectors with high investment costs, where the risks could prove fatal. Such risks can be reduced by external participation in the cost of the R&D performed or purchased. This is external subsidizing (internal is from the firm's own resources). The external subsidizing is normally preferable to the industry, as it does not weaken their market position, and allows them to continue the work without impairing their profitability (often the key for further growth). In knowledge intensive sectors, R&D subsidies are easier to find than any other kind of subsidy. These subsidies are more prevalent than marketing or other subsidies, and also tend to cover a higher ratio of the relevant expense. There are many different mechanisms and schemes for that purpose on regional, national, and supra-national levels. There are subsidies for knowledge purchase, for joint development of the knowledge (Eureka), bi-national funds and agreements for funding. There are the "do–it–yourself" support mechanisms and the many partner mechanisms (EU Framework Program's). The programs either fully subsidize the R&D by supporting it, or loan the funds to be returned later on—normally giving better than market conditions—where even the waiving of collateral is an improvement.

Absorb the Costs and Reduce Profits

There is a strong argument for the strategy in which no administrative burden is placed on the firm, nor any strain on its market position. There is a basic requirement of course, and that is the financial viability of the firm. Only firms which have the financial ability to withstand such a strategy (this does not refer to a single occurrence or to a short-term step) can elect this strategy. The source for absorbing the cost can be either from the firm's capital, devaluation of the firm's value (or stock value) or through the firm's reduction in profits. While start-up firms who may feel less pressure to show great profit may opt for the usage of the income as the source, and may also shy from reducing the stock value, while the other more veteran firms may be more sensitive to their profit stream. The only problem is that the reduced profits put the livelihood of the firm at risk in the long run, as well as, use the capital. Neither solution seems to fit the long-term viability and health of the company, while short-term solutions may depend on sector custom or the age of the firm. More philosophically, since the firm is created with the intent of economic gain, such a move goes against this basic argument.

BASIC TERMS

Here I will be introducing the definitions of the most important terms to be used throughout the book, even if the theoretical basis is not defined in that specific chapter. The world of Collaborative Research is rich in definitions and terms. Up to this point, when using an external source, the terms used by the source were depicted, as defined by the source. From this point onwards, in order to keep the discussion clear, a unified definition system seems to be required. For additional clarity, the terms to be used in the discussion hereafter, have been elaborated on in the following list. They are to be understood in the sense defined in the following section, unless stated otherwise.

Terms and Definitions

1. **Collaborative Research (CR):** Research performed in collaboration between different partners, each owning

research capabilities and are able to execute their part in the combined research plan, towards owning a combined or compatible technology, which could lead to joint products or compatible products. Collaborative research is jointly directed and the results are evaluated in cooperation. CR may be performed under an agreement or through a jointly owned legal entity, with internal (of the partners) or external funding. Each partner performs the research for its own ends, while it may enjoy research results achieved by the others, at least some of its work must be for each partner's own benefit (sub-contracting is not collaborative research). It may also be performed among exclusively industrial partners; however, in most cases the reference in this book will be to a group consisting industry (users) and research organizations (providers).

2. **R&D Consortia:** The partners for a research organism that performs the research on behalf of the partners. The consortium will perform the research sometimes using its own personnel or personnel "loaned" by the partners. The research results are jointly owned and so are the utilization rights. A central lab which will perform the research is optional. The consortium may be formed as a legal entity or just by contract.

3. **RJV (Research Joint Venture):** Each partner will perform one's own part of the research project, using its facilities (existing or created for the project) and resources, and will own the knowledge it develops. The utilization rights are allocated according to a pre-arranged agreement, settling the obligations and rights of each partner.

4. **SRJV (Structured Research Joined Venture):** A Research Joint Venture (RJV), under a structured program, on a regional, national, or supra-national authority which supervises the proceedings to promote its own end, and sometime funds the joint ventures to pre-defined extent.

5. **Central Laboratory:** The R&D in the grouped organization is performed in a central location, and not individually at the premises of the partners or by their personnel. The personnel performing the work can be employees of

one of the partners, sub-contractors, or be employed by a legal entity forming the partnership of the involved stakeholders. The existence of the central laboratory requires a clear and well-understood ownership and sharing mechanism regarding the research results.

6. **Cross Licensing Agreements (CLAs):** In the CLA, the partners sign an agreement to let each one use the knowledge of the others and pay the others', users fee. In addition, if there is any sub-licensing agreement, the original owners of the knowledge will be compensated. In the CLA, each partner has the incentive to give his knowledge to the others, with the knowledge that they will maximize their revenues.

7. **Intellectual Property (IP):** The definition of knowledge whether tangible or not in a specific form (patent, trademarks, and so on). The IP will be a tangible form of an intangible item.

8. **Intellectual Property Rights (IPR):** The legal rights related to the IP, whether ipso-facto or ex-ante to the creation of the IP. Thus, a licensing agreement for a patent would be IPR as it would grant rights. A research agreement describing the access right to any future resulting IP, would also be IPR.

9. **Publication:** The appearance of the knowledge in academic or trade magazines, books or news announcements, or in presentations at conferences. Patents are excluded from this definition, as is the incorporation of the knowledge inside a product.

10. **Patent:** Either a single patent or a family of patents. There will be no distinction for the purposes of this book, unless explicitly so declared.

SUMMARY

As we have seen, the industry in knowledge-based sectors is required to invest in R&D in order to survive, and to further promote its position. There are industrial sectors where, due to the short life cycle of the products, the fast advance of technology, and the pressure to reduce costs result in a situation where R&D expenses run very high. Firms facing the R&D race theoretically have three options, but of them only one is really viable (for small, as well as, large firms) in the long term: subsidizing the R&D cost from external sources. Luckily, such sources exist, and seem to be prolific in research intensive sectors. However, finance probably does not answer all, and here is where Collaborative Research and the academy enter.

The definitions of the terms to be used in the following chapters have also been given. We are now ready to discuss the role of R&D and CR in company life.

3
Forms of Collaborative Research

This chapter will introduce the topic of collaboration in research, and the different methods for performing that cooperation. The different methods such as, solitary research, R&D Consortia, and RJV (see Chapter 2) will be described and analyzed. A comparison between Free RJV and SRJV is presented, as well as, the economic justification for financially supporting RJVs will be provided. Two examples of support given to SRJV is described (Magnet Program and the EU Framework Program), in support of the economic point of view that the RJV and the SRJV are more beneficial to society than other forms of generic R&D. Towards the end of the chapter I have compared the advantages and disadvantages of the different methods.

THE TRIPLE HELIX

It is impossible to discuss the interaction among government, industry and academy on an academic level without mentioning the Triple Helix concept (Etzkowitz and Leydersdorrf, 1997; Etzkowitz, 1999). The Triple Helix concept deals with the interaction among the three players, and sees their actions as co-dependent and influencing each other, and the environment they are active in, is too wide for the purpose of this book. It is assumed for the purpose of this book that the influence the academy and industry have on the government is not relevant to the point of making the government realize that the CR encouragement programs are important, and would have a positive influence on the economy. The resulting role of the government can be positive—supportive of such programs; or neutral—that is, neither supporting nor prohibiting CR; or negative—prohibiting or discouraging CR. The basic assumption in this book is that CR will be beneficial for all participants. Therefore, it is assumed that the relevant government will know that, and will endeavor at least to be neutral, if not fully positive. The rest of the discussion, up to the government chapter, will focus on the Academy–Industry interaction.

THE PLACE OF R&D AND CR IN FIRM ACTIVITY

While CR is the focus of discussion in this book, it is rarely the main focus of a firm. In order to better understand the real role of CR for the partners, it would be necessary to better understand the role of generic R&D for firms. If we start with a question: What is the role of R&D in firms? We may get several answers [the role of R&D is to allow firms to assimilate knowledge (Kamien et al., 1992; Kamien and Zang, 2000)]. The obvious answer would be to create the technologies and products with which later on the firm will generate sales and therefore income (see Figure 3.1 and Figure 3.2). The obvious would be to see R&D as the creation of a strategic resource for the firm (Cabral, 2000), the basis for products and therefore income leading to profits, that is, the ultimate end of the firm. The role of research as a strategic activity is of course intensified in knowledge-based sectors, rather than in others. Other activities like marketing, financing, and productions, for example, could be more important in these sectors. However, we will claim that there is much more to be gained by R&D.

The analysis of spillovers (Katsoulacos and Ulph, 1998) has shown that without R&D, firms just do not manage to acquire new technologies. It is very clear that the firms require the R&D capability to be able to translate non-industrial or non-firm knowledge into something the production and maintenance functions in the firm can relate to, and utilizes. This is the function of the R&D unit of a firm, and without it, not only will the firm create no knowledge of its own, but it will have a problem in the translation, as there is no unit in it with the expertise or duty to do so. But how important is that function really?

Figure 3.1: R&D Interaction with Firm Function

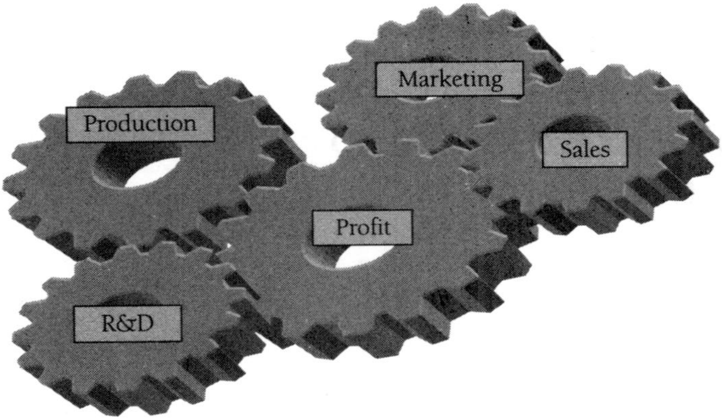

Source: Author's own.

An Alternative:

Figure 3.2: Role of Generic R&D

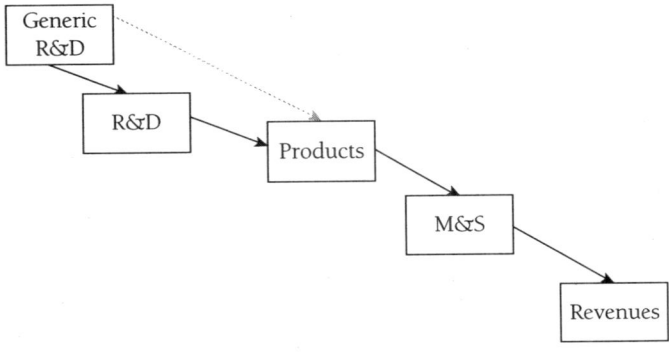

Source: Author's own.

In the Low-Tech sectors, the benefits of R&D, especially generic R&D, are only for the long term, and even just in the move into other sectors. As discussed earlier, we are dealing with the short life cycle product sectors and the High-Tech sectors, where the R&D function is extremely important. During the 1990s, we have seen firms buying other firms in order to acquire technologies that they had no other way of assimilating. A special example is the 1980s and 1990s activity in the pharmaceuticals sector, where the large firms merged or acquired the small, fast, and innovative Bio-Tech firms in order to cope with the changes in the pharmaceuticals business. The example of the pharmaceuticals firms is especially relevant to our estimation of the importance of the generic R&D. The generic R&D is most relevant for a firm interested in developing new disciplinary capabilities. It is very difficult for a firm to incorporate a new disciplinary capability into product development without a strong generic basis. As the High-Tech sectors are becoming more and more multi-disciplinary, generic R&D is gaining importance in these fields.

Accepting the importance of generic R&D, why would an industrial company elect generic R&D with the Academy?

If we understand the increasing importance of generic R&D in gaining access and acquiring multi-disciplinary abilities for the firms, the answer is almost elementary enough for a layman to understand. First, generic R&D is closest to basic research than it is to development, and thus it is something the academy excels at, making it a good partner to learn from and cooperate with. Moreover, as it contains an element of teaching some of the basics of the new discipline that is also something the academy does on a daily basis, making it an even more attractive partner. But the most attractive element in cooperating with the academy is the reduced strategic risk as the academy is not going to compete with the firm in the market or in future markets, and at the same time provide a good support basis for further work. Further on, the academy is characterized by free flow of basic knowledge, which means that the firm connected to it can enjoy that characteristic when trying to solve multi-disciplinary problems. It only has to take care that its own knowledge is blocked from that free flow.[7]

---

[7] There is obviously a down side to that. See Chapter 8.

R&D COLLABORATION FORMS

Collaborative Research can take several forms. These forms will be further described in this chapter, as well as, the special interest area: the Academia–Industry Collaborative Research, which introduces the topic of cooperation in research.

Forms of Collaborative Research (Kamien and Zang, 2000):

1. Solitary R&D: The individual firm performs its own R&D to its own ends. In this case, the firm has conflicting goals regarding the development and usage of the knowledge, as this knowledge is not shared.
2. RJV (Research Joint Venture): (see Chapter 2)
3. R&D Consortium: (see Chapter 2)
4. CLA (Cross Licensing Agreement): (see Chapter 2)

In their article, Kamien and Zang (2000) show that the social benefit is positive for all four forms, but that it is in fact, greatest for the RJV. However, the different forms and their analysis do not show the most interesting factor; the Academia–Industry conflict.

SOLITARY R&D

This is the most basic and prevalent form of R&D and can be found in all sectors and in all countries in small, medium, and multi-national size firms. The results of the research can be private or public and can be used or shelved (not used), all according to the discretion of the firm performing the R&D. This form of R&D is less interesting for this book, as the purpose here is to analyze the interaction between a specific partnership, that is, the Academy–Industry partnership, which does not exist in solitary R&D.

Box 3.1: Solitary R&D

A firm identifies the need in the market for an improved, smaller, more efficient power source for portable devices. The firm has access to the required knowledge and launches an internal development project, using

Contd. Box 3.1

Contd. Box 3.1

> input from marketing, as well as engineering (for example, characterization, standardization requirements and so on). The resulting product is fully-owned by the firm, and once it is integrated into other systems, it results in economic benefits to the firm, making it a significant income source for it.
>
> A firm in pharmaceuticals purchased a basic patent (patent family) for a specific substance to be used as a drug. The firm commences the long process of turning the substance into an approved of marketing drug, investing heavily in the process of FDA approval via clinical trials. Once the drug is approved, the patenting allows the firm to reap huge revenues, increasing its wealth and bringing huge profits to its shareholders.

RJV (RESEARCH JOINT VENTURE)

The RJV is typically fitting partners with an existing research infrastructure. This form of R&D can be found under two specific sub-species: the Free RJV and the Structured RJV (SRJV). The Free RJV or RJV is a voluntary agreement between at least two interested partners seeking to benefit from the arrangement. The SRJV will be similar but will involve a supporting authority, interested in fostering the cooperation, and who may be involved in the RJV; normally not in the research itself but at least in the management. The RJV in general will have the following advantages:

1. It will allow all partners to retain and to a certain extent develop their research abilities.
2. It will reduce development costs as research is shared between partners and the scope of research covered is wider than would optimally be expected from a single firm (Kamien and Zang, 2000)
3. As confidentiality may be imposed at any time, it is deemed necessary, and access can be restricted to any "knowledge", each partner may retain as confidential, any part of knowledge (he owns or develops) that is not related to the RJV. The firms need reveal only the knowledge promised at the outset of the project.

The RJV however has some weak points as well:

1. Each partner has little control over the research performed by the others.
2. Coordination of the joint research is difficult.
3. Research abilities in new disciplines owned by the other partners are hard to copy.

Box 3.2: The Free RJV—the US Model

Since 1984, the US National Cooperation Research Act, has allowed firms wishing to collaborate in R&D, to do so, without fear of retribution by the anti-trust laws, conditioned on their registering that collaboration with the ministry of industry and trade. Formerly, such cooperation was deemed as a form of market collusion, and was therefore problematic. The firms decide between themselves—in most cases, there are only two firms (Olk, 1991)—the mechanisms for coordination of research, and resources dedicated by each partner and so on.

The main benefit of the Free RJV is that, it allows the firms to determine the topic and the management of the research. There are no minimum or maximum of resources to be invested; and except for the anti-trust issue, there is no external control, or need in reporting.

Box 3.3: The Structured RJV

In 1985, the EU Commission (Miyagiwa and Ohno, 2002) opened the SRJV called EU Framework Programs for Research (EU Framework Program). The EU Framework Program can be taken, according to scope of disciplines, topics, and size (expressed by budgets, number of participants and duration in years) as the anti-thesis for the Free RJV. Currently (2007–2013), the Seventh Framework Program is in operation with a total budget of over 21 billion Euros for the period.

There are many other different forms of the SRJV, but as this program has all the common characteristics, as well as, some unique features, it was selected as a counter for Free RJV.

The EU Framework Program is managed on a supra-national level, with (in Framework Program 6) 33 participating countries. It includes participants from the academia, industry and other bodies.

Contd. Box 3.3

Contd. Box 3.3

> An SRJV, in contrast with a Free RJV contributes financial support to the RJVs selected. This contribution requires more involvement on the side of the supporting agency (the EU Commission in that case) than the mere registration of the Free RJV. It requires submission of a proposal to be approved according to submission rules and evaluation rules, the signing of a contract with the funding agency, and later monitoring and reporting (evaluated as well) to approve the funding.

As an SRJV in contract to Free RJV, the EU Framework Program is intended for promoting the goals and reaching the targets of the funding agency. Some of these targets have nothing to do with the technological or disciplinary aspects of the R&D (such as promoting women or small medium enterprises). The additional agenda is expressed in the management of the projects and the rules for participation, as well as, in the topics selected for promotion. Moreover, when the operating agency deems that there are technologies, or, topics it wants to promote, without sufficient interest, it uses actions designed to generate interest in these topics or technologies.[8] While the Free RJV is by nature Bottom–Up, when selecting the topics and disciplines involved, as well as, the number and nature of participants, the EU Framework Program is not so. It is the EU commission that selects the topics to be presented in the calls, and the types of projects to be used for each. The nature and number of participants are typical to the tools selected. The SRJV is the epitomization of the Top–Down approach.

While this discussion deals with the reasons for the increased administrative burden (Porath, 2004), the motive is the financial constraints, enhanced by the controls enforced on the executive agency. Over 21 billion Euros may seem formidable, but with a ration of proposals to funding at over 10:1, it is clearly not so. Moreover, the financial and administrative controls enforced on the EU Commission, require that the EU Commission show that the funding is spent

---

[8]SSA—Specific Support Action is such a pre-designed tool to generate research interest, as well as, create input for commission decisions, and prepare roadmaps towards following EU Framework Programs.

wisely and fairly (most beneficial way to the public and in accordance with EU policies). In their article Yun, Park and Ahn (2000)[9] claim that under moderate competition, it is for the general good or social benefit, if the firms use RJV (as defined here), however, it is less beneficial for the firms themselves. Therefore, they recommend that governing bodies or agencies subsidize this activity to make it more attractive for the industry to join. Their recommendation, that in very competitive fields, independent R&D is most beneficial, ignores the special conditions of specific sectors in which basic research is very costly, while at the same time being close to the final product, as seen in the development process. This is the economic viewpoint justification for the SRJV.

> **Box 3.4: Magnet Program–SRJV**
>
> In the example of the Israeli Magnet Program (described in details in the appendix to this chapter), the role of the Research Organization is built into the program rules of participation. Unlike the Framework Program in the Magnet Program Research Consortia, the participation of a Research Organization is obligatory. However, the identity of the specific Research Organization or the industrial partners is of course, not specified in the rules. The participation in the program is encouraged via economic support, as well as the access (under preferable conditions) to the research facilities and research results. In the EU Framework Program similarly there is a financial incentive as well as the access to leading researchers, research facilities and research results that the program gives.
>
> In both these cases, the financial incentive is in the form of grant (in fact in Framework Program 7, the former "financial support" has been changed into "Grant" and the term "Proposer" into "Grant Applicants"), which is not to be paid back. The grant ratio from the overall budget is also relatively high, which is another characteristic of generic R&D.

The SRJV has therefore the advantage of the financing it gets from the executing agency. The research performed by each firm while coordinating effort with the others—compared to the Free RJV (see Table 3.1)—is regulated most of the time by

---

[9]They define the terms RJV and R&D Consortium differently, from the way we do.

topics, partners (number and type), time, and additional agendas of the agency involved. Today, with the increasing trend of investing in innovation, and therefore in R&D, and the wish of governments to push in that direction,[10] the SRJV is becoming ever more common around the world.

Table 3.1: Free RJV vs. SRJV Summary

Characteristic	Free RJV	SRJV
Selection of topics/disciplines	Bottom–Up	Top–Down/Bottom–Up
Participants number and type	Free	Pre-selected according to rules
Management structure	Free	According to participation rules
Minimum/maximum investment of resources and types of resources invested in project	According to agreement among partners	Predetermined by rules and financing agency
Level of involvement of financing/monitoring agency	Minimum	At least periodical reporting, checking adherence to original plan of action and to general financial guidelines
Level of financial support	None	Depending on the nature of the project and the type of partner.
External administrative burden	Minimal	Medium to heavy, depending on the complexity and intensity of the reporting and proposal preparation.

Source: Based on author's own research.

R&D CONSORTIUM

Unlike the RJV, in the consortium, research is done jointly. If it is an industrial consortium and the research is sub-contracted to the

---

[10]The most known is the Barcelona Declaration with its update (http://ac.europa.eu/growthandjobs/faqs/background/index_en.htm)

academy, then we are dealing with a contracted research (see the Section on "Other Forms of Academy–Industry Cooperation"). However, between academy and industry, the R&D consortium will probably include some academic research. In most probability if there is a central lab, it may be located at the academic institute site in order to even allow accessibility to all industrial partners and reduce the fears of opportunism. The R&D consortium has the following advantages:

1. It allows cost reductions by actually sharing the research costs among the partners.
2. It allows the partners to continue other R&D projects they may have without fear of spillover.
3. The potential for continued cooperation is easily promoted, as the site for it already exists, and relational assets are easy to build.
4. If the consortium forms the research activity as a legal entity and allows it to own the knowledge, then that entity may later on be commercialized as a spin-off.

The consortium requires that the firms invest in the research unit; the higher the sunk cost, the higher the tendency of the consortium members to try and prolong its use. This is done by either making the unit a joint research center for longer periods, or trying to make it a profit center. However, the R&D Consortium has some weak points:

1. Establishing the entity for research is a complicated administrative task (unless there is a supervising authority setting the rules and lowering the administrative burden). The establishment of the central research is a significant sunk cost for all partners.
2. The Consortium can create a research unit that will demand continuation even when the circumstances require something else. Dismantling the unit is also very problematic in terms of sharing the remains.
3. The ownership and management of the research results can be complicated. The partners may wish to define ownership and right of use to their advantage.

4. Creation of relational assets among the partners, and not between each partner and the research unit may be slow in development.

Box 3.5: Mechanics Consortium

> In order to overcome the manufacturing problems in mechanics, several firms in the same section decide to share the cost and contract a close university laboratory with a specialty in mechanics. The unit is contracted on behalf of the R&D Consortium and the consortium members share the cost. The results are also to be jointly shared by all the Consortium members, and none has the right to sub-contract them outside the group, without the consent of all the other members.
>
> The unit performs the research under the supervision of a committee of the consortium members. The knowledge is shared by the members who use it in their manufacturing routines. Once the research is over, the Consortium is dissolved and the members turn to their own business.
>
> The research unit continues to perform research in the field but does not publish the results of the research performed for the Consortium.

CROSS LICENSING AGREEMENT (CLA)

The CLA is an array of license agreements among the R&D partners, allowing each the use of the knowledge received from the others under certain economic (royalties) conditions. The CLA allows each partner to pursue their own research agenda, and co-ordinates the research effort so that each partner can maximize the potential of its research abilities and strengths, while enjoying the fruits of the partner's efforts. This way the partners can each invest in the development of the technologies they are best at, knowing they will have to pay for the use of the other partners' technologies which will be made available to them under known conditions, and not bear the cost of the development of these technologies (Pastor and Sandonis, 2002).

Due to the nature of the CLA, it is better suited for Industry–Industry cooperation. A partnership in which each partner has something to give and something to gain, without an increase in the cost, that is, a partnership between beneficiaries of the same nature. The CLA will allow the academy little benefit over a simple licensing agreement, as the academy has no direct way of using the knowledge developed by the industry for profit making. The only benefit derived by the academy from industrial knowledge will be in further research, and for that purpose the CLA is an over shoot.

The CLA has the following positive points:

1. It allows real sharing of the knowledge as each partner gains from the use the other partners make of its knowledge.
2. The costs of the research are shared in a way similar to the RJV.
3. Each partner maintains the use of its research facilities and abilities similar to the RJV.
4. Similar to the RJV, each partner retains confidentiality regarding the other research projects it performs.

However, it also has the following weak points:

1. Each partner has little control over the research performed by the others.
2. The CLA may require the partner to expose the deals it makes when utilizing knowledge originating from the other partners.
3. Research abilities in new disciplines owned by the other partners are hard to copy.

Box 3.6: CLA

Two firms decide to coordinate their effort in the development of new Very Large Scale Integrated Circuits (VLSI) technologies. Each firm has its own unique capabilities and so they sign Cross Licensing Agreement (CLA), allowing each the use of the others technology up to a certain level without royalty, and from a certain point, with fixed royalty. The firms have reduced R&D expenses as they can coordinate their research effort and make sure the technologies are compatible without having each firm

Contd. Box 3.6

Contd. Box 3.6

> develop the full technology itself, resulting in doubling the development effort, while getting the same end result. Since each partner is focusing on their strengths, they make fewer mistakes in development and progress is faster and cheaper. At the end of the project, both firms are ready with the next generation of products, and have a strategic advantage over the competitors in the market.

OTHER FORMS OF ACADEMY-INDUSTRY COOPERATION

In addition to the forms mentioned above, Academy–Industry cooperation can take other forms which preclude cooperation in research. Such forms as Technology Transfer, Contracted Research and others are based on the assumption that all or nearly all of the research is performed by the academy, while the industry is mostly a recipient of the results, whether by determining the scope before the research or ipso-facto.

Licensing

This is the most prevalent form of Technology Transfer in existence, and it is a source of intensive effort at national and institutional levels to improve the results of this activity. The academy develops the knowledge by itself through an independent research. This knowledge is transferred to the industry—which is why often this is referred to as TT (Technology Transfer)—and normally to one firm for utilization under a contract. The knowledge is usually protected by patents or other protection. The license agreement defines the knowledge and the uses the licensee can put that knowledge to. This form of activity in which the academy develops the knowledge based on curiosity and un-directed research, suffers from an inherent fault, and that is, that the knowledge is by definition and origin not fitting industrial use. Since the knowledge was created based on curiosity, it normally lacks (among other things) economic considerations, adherence to standards, and other factors relevant for the intended use. Another major fault lies in the fact that in many cases, knowledge developed while answering questions of scientific importance has no answers to the market needs that is required by firms. Even knowledge intensive firms tend to baulk at knowledge that would not give them any significant marketing advantage over their competition. Adding to that, the fact that the licensing agreement demand that the patent protection be kept and that the industry make use (for the benefit of the public) of the knowledge, additional heavy costs and obligations are incurred, making firms shy away from this form.

Contracted Research

The Industry defines the research scope and the expected outcomes, and pays a fee to the academy for the work involved. In this sub-contractor like activity, the Academy normally retains no Intellectual Property; only the industry owns the knowledge. This is not a real collaboration as the industry does not share any information with the Academy, and there is no joint invention. These would normally fit more research institutes, when and where available. However, this form of joint activity, overcomes several faults: the licensing, the research and its results (assuming the research is successful) will be ready for use by the industry, complete from the utilizations point of view and intended to give the firm the competitive advantage it requires, and have economic relevance, as well as, standardization aspects that the firm deems important.

However, this form of cooperation is not the primary focus for discussion in this book. The reasons for that are:

1. There is no joint work between the two partners.
2. The deals seem to be more in the nature of a purchase than of a joint project. The relations between the partners are of the client–supplier type.

3. The incidental nature of the event prevents, in most cases, the creation of long-term relational assets. It is harder to expect this to lead to long-term relationships.

ADVANTAGES AND DISADVANTAGES OF DIFFERENT COLLABORATION FORMS

As the sections above mentioned, each form of cooperation has its own positive points. The forms of cooperation normally fit different situations and sectors.

While the topic of Technology Transfer (TT) is very interesting and a lot of activity is on-going, both in theory and in practice (*Journal for Technology Transfer* is evidence of that), it is not the central theme for this book. However, as TT or licensing of Knowledge developed in the Academy independently from the Industry is prevalent,[11] it requires some referring too. This book concentrates on Collaborative Research, intended to allow the industry to enjoy more than just the academic knowledge. CR allows for the transfer of disciplinary capability as well as concrete knowledge. It affords the academy to work towards the industry interested in directions and allows the industry to learn the basis. It is true, that in CR, there is an element of TT. If your focus point is TT, than CR is a private case of TT; if the Collaboration is your focus then the TT is merely a tool for deriving a major benefit from the CR. When performing *pure TT*, there is always the problem of overcoming the gap that is not an easy hurdle to get over, and when combined with irrelevant research direction, forms the bulk of failed TT. Boxes 3.7 and 3.8, demonstrate just how destructive that gap can be.

Yet another problem, is the expectation of universities and other research institutes, to make a profit out of TT. The unique

---

[11]The Israeli universities led by the Weitzman Institute and the Hebrew University have made huge profits from such activities, and per their size are leading in the world in royalties.

examples of success encourage that expectation. However, it does not work all the time, and hardly ever in the short term, as is revealed when delving deeper into the success stories. The large expense incurred by the Technology Transfer Office (TTO) or the Technology Transfer Company (TTC) is hard to eclipse in most cases.

The advantage CR offers is double. The direction of research interests the industry and increases the chances of successful licensing, else they would not participate, and the industry also assures that it will be able to overcome the gap either by the CR or independently by training and acquiring the relevant skills. Moreover, with most financing mechanisms offered in SRJVs today, the costs of the TTO/TTC both for research and for IPR protection are covered. More will be discussed later in this book.

Box 3.7: Low-tech Example

A Low-tech firm in a well established market was introduced to a Technology Transfer Office of a university via the national association for its sector. The association was approached by the TTO to try and market a technology developed in the university through basic research. The firm had no R&D department. In the past, the firm would buy equipment for its processes and would get also support and instruction for its use with the installation service. For the cooperation, the researchers attached to the project from the university side, helped the firm identify potential R&D personnel from the production department and started instructing them in the formation of the research lab to be able to absorb the university knowledge. The process was difficult; there were no internal routines as how to interface between the department and other departments/functions in the firm, and while the technology was transferred, its implementation did not go well, and the technology was discarded. Sometime later the R&D department was disbanded.

Box 3.8: Long-term Research

In a large R&D consortium, the industry decided to dedicate some funds for long-term research, without visible usage at the time. Several proposals from the academy were identified and selected. One of the proposals ended with results that could be useful for a specific firm in the R&D

Contd. Box 3.8

Contd. Box 3.8

> consortium, but the usage was not clear, and was not entered into the firm's work schedule. Although negotiations between the firm and the academic institute involved progressed up to an understanding and an MOU, the firm while trying to retain the rights to the knowledge, refused to commit to actually licensing it. The process lasted several years, making the technology slowly obsolete and creating dissatisfaction on both sides.

SUMMARY

The main aim of this chapter was to introduce the topic of collaboration in research, and the different methods for performing that cooperation. The different methods such as, solitary research, R&D Consortia, and RJV were described and analyzed.

A comparison between Free RJV and SRJV is presented, as well as, the economic justification for financially supporting RJVs. Two examples of support given to SRJV were described (Magnet Program and the EU Framework Program), in support of the economic point of view that the RJV and the SRJV are more beneficial to society than other forms of Generic R&D.

Also, more remote collaboration methods such as Licensing and Contracted Research were described and analyzed. The faults of Licensing based on basic research in the academy were described, as were those of Contracted Research, leading to the advantages of Collaborative Research over the two.

The last section compared the advantages and disadvantages of the different methods. Following this introduction of the different forms of CR, Chapter 4 will present some models of CR activities.

APPENDIX

The Israeli Magnet Program

The data source selected in this case is the Israeli Magnet Program. This program (see www.magnet.org.il) has its own influence on the suggested model, but the changes required will fit many other SRJV programs. The explanation will begin with a presentation of the stages of the formation and establishment of SRJV under the program, and will then move to the functions. The stages follow the process from top to bottom.

The process of a Magnet consortium formation begins with a submission of an initiation document by a group of entrepreneurs to the manager of the Magnet Authority, responsible for the management of the program. The manager then institutes a very short preliminary examination stage in which he determines the value of launching the process. He may consult advisers or his staff before making that decision. Once that decision is made, the Magnet Authority will issue a public call for participation in a Kick-Off meeting. That call is published in two leading business magazines and to a specific target audience (the research universities). In the Kick-Off meeting, the entrepreneurs present their initiative and the other participants present their interests and contributions. In that meeting or shortly after it, the working group is formed that will prepare and submit by a predetermined deadline, the preliminary proposal called *General Justification Document*. That document is brought, after evaluation, to the Magnet Committee, and the selected groups are requested to submit the full proposal called *Detailed Justification Document*. That document will go through evaluation as per the work program, the budget, and the eligibility of the participants to take part in the SRJV project. The expected products and their national and sectoral impacts are evaluated. During the evaluation (when there is a positive indication of approval), the Magnet Authority will *hint* to the groups that they should proceed to establishing the legal entity (a not-for-profit association). The evaluation results will be forwarded to the Magnet committee (the advisory body of the authority for the programs it controls) that will approve the program and the work is launched.

The formation process can be divided, for the purpose of this book, into two main stages: pre-Kick-Off Meeting, and following it. If the initial group fails to reach the Kick-Off Meeting, no consortium will be formed. However, reaching it still requires other steps to be successful. It is after the Kick-Off Meeting that the Domain Consensus has to be reached, in order to proceed. In the Structured Program (SP) model (see Figure 3A.1), the parameters leading to the Kick-Off Meeting are considered to lead to the Domain Consensus.

Figure 3A.1: The Israeli Magnet Approval Process

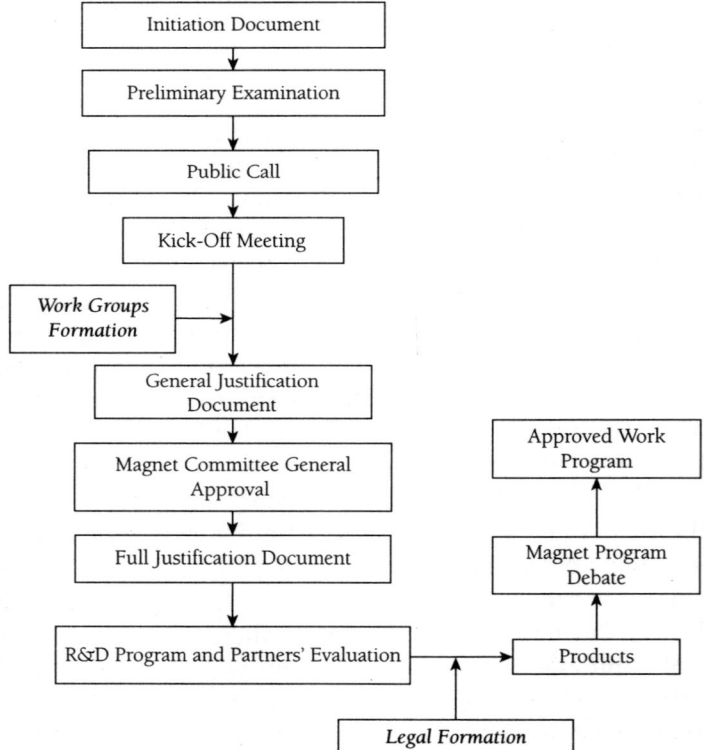

Source: Based on a presentation of the Magnet Authority (adapted and modified).

4
The Multi-dimensional Model

This chapter will focus on the CR model. The roles of the different participants will be described, as well as, their interaction and the multi-dimensional model will be presented. The first stage in understanding CR is realizing that it is a multi-dimensional activity. While in most cases in management papers, there is a tendency to try and reduce analysis into a two dimensional analysis for the sake of clarification, in the case of SRJV, I feel that trying to describe the activity on a 2×2 matrix would result in a misleading, poor description and even poorer understanding.

The SRJV has several participants (with a degenerated form of two partners–duo analysis) dealing with science–technology issues, but having economic implications regarding these issues, and potential results (Intellectual Property [IP]) with important legal aspects (Intellectual Property Rights [IPR]). Since the CR is a cooperation activity, it is important to understand the role of the different participants in CR as a basis to understanding it. The Academy and Industry introduce the multi-cultural aspect—internationality of players can only add to that—and the introduction of the government (even under a Triple Helix description) only complicates the issue further. Therefore, economics, organizational aspects, legal aspects, financial aspects, issues of governance, and the role of Government in economic development (via the Triple Helix point of analysis) are all relevant. Moreover, all are time-relevant and, therefore, require analyzing simultaneously in order to get a correct picture.

So how can a comprehensive multi-dimensional model be constructed and yet be understandable?

R&D DEFINITION

R&D is a complex process and displays much variety, differing from one industrial sector to another, as well as, within sectors. Research and Development (R&D), is made up of two very different actions which can be generalized in the following manner:

Research

It is a *search for the better understanding of a phenomena or an observation*. It also includes the search for the parameters influencing the observation, and the manner in which they are affecting it. Research may involve an element of innovation, both in the methods used, the disciplines involved and the explanation offered. It can extend into models and prototypes trying to simulate the operation of the observation. However, research does not deal with the market applications and marketing optimization of the innovation. Research is the activity performed mainly by the academy and research institutions.

Development

It is the *search for the optimal market solution for a product or a service*. Development takes into account the final use of the innovation and invention, and tries to make science meet the real world. In development, parameters, such as cost, marketing demands, and standards are taken into account. It may be based on discoveries and innovations resulting from research. This process is performed mostly by the industry, and it leads to the appearance of products and services. Even though research has a clear scientific affiliation, development can be technology agnostic, leaning towards a sort of business solution. In this aspect, the definition here is close to innovation. Therefore, from this point onwards, development will also be read as innovation.

Therefore, it may be understood that the two actions are linked and connected, and that the transition from one to the other is gradual, while differentiation is somewhat artificial. There are many stages in the R&D process, and while the definition of the stages may seem clear, the boundaries are seldom so. The move from basic research to applied research is difficult to identify. However, in most cases when the academy is involved, it may be safely assumed that the R&D has a strong element of research, and is therefore more of Applied Research. This means, that it is in the research domain but closer to development, where uses and potential market demands are influencing the work; and the role of innovation is more dominant than the search for better understanding. However, this type of research is normally more general, in the technology level, and less regarding actual products. The CR described in this book deals with this type of research, the most prevalent meeting point between the Academy and the Industry. There are other less frequent partnerships—with either more basic research, or with some actual development—but these are rare, and at least in the field of product development very rarely is there more than one industrial partner.

DIMENSIONS OF THE MODEL

Understanding the model first requires mapping the different dimensions, and then presenting the basic assumptions to proceed from.

Legal[12]

The legal dimension of the CR can be divided into a generic central part (the IPR and related topics) and the framework (legal entity formed aspects of the agreement between the partners and so on). The framework aspects were also briefly touched upon while discussing the different forms of CR. It is therefore of less

---

[12]The IP aspect will be further expanded in Chapter 7. At this point the legal dimension will be dealt with in a general form.

importance here. The main issue is the generic central part of the legal dimension, as this one is both crucial for the success or failure of the CR, and is also a major reason for starting it. It is the main contention of this book, that the basic, most important reason for CR is the creation of usable knowledge. There are financial and relational assets and motives involved, but they are of lesser significance. The generic aspect relates to two main items under the IPR: the ownership and access rights to the IP. The analysis unit of the model in that perspective is to check whether the ownership and access rights awarded, fit the goals of the governing body creating the CR environment, the goals and aims of the partners and their expectations. In order to be able to assess it, the model will introduce a third parameter, that is, the clarity of the IPR. It is a major hurdle for the long-term existence of any CR program if the IPR are unclear, or open to interpretation by the players. The legal dimension can be described as follows: (see Table 4.1)

Table 4.1: Legal Parameters of the Model[13]

Parameter	Positive	Negative
Clarity of IPR		
Fit of ownership to players expectations and goals		
Fit of access rights to players expectations and goals		
General legal environment influence		

Source: Author's own.

Clarity of the IPR

This denotes the level of certainty for all partners regarding their ability to achieve their technological/economic goals. This section refers to the level the IPR are clear to the participants.

---

[13]This table is presented as template to be filled in by the user/reader.

Players

The different players are further analyzed in the following sections where the description will be limited to their aspects affecting the model.

Government

The government is the only player interested in promoting the play, not for the direct benefits potentially derived from it, but rather from either the existence of the play itself (it is doing something), or future secondary economic results, and is, therefore, a leading player though somewhat strange. The government is playing the *big numbers game* while also being interested in specific success stories to help it market the game. On the other hand, the government has a specific interest to show that *fair play* and transparency regarding public funds and their allocation has been maintained. The government may be defined as a player, by creating the CR environment, but it does not necessarily have an active role in the management of the project, at most, it has a supervisory role. The involvement of the government can therefore be analyzed according to the following parameters (see Table 4.2):

Table 4.2: Players' (Government) Parameters[14]

Parameter	Positive	Negative
Clarity of IPR		
Administrative burden		
Amount of instructions		
Amount of annual reporting		
Level of support		
Program insistence on results		
Other parameters		

Source: Author's own.

---

[14] This table is presented as template to be filled in by the user/reader.

Administrative Burden

This is the level of involvement of the governing agency. It is measured according to the following criteria:

1. Amount of instructions for the preparation of the proposal before submission: heavy, medium, light.
2. Amount of annual reporting: Once (light), every six months and deliverables (medium), and quarterly or monthly and deliverables (heavy).
3. Level of support, such as, financing (percentage of the budget), part that is given as grant, preferred loan, etc.
4. Program insistence on results expressed, as the results are required for the project design by the program impact assurance system. Is there a demand to see utilization (or else penalty)? What kind of commitment is required from the participants?
5. Other parameters, such as, the level of freedom for budget changes within the budget frame, and participation of agency representatives in management or technical meetings.

Academy

The Academy[15] is a necessary participant in any CR. This player is mostly interested in specific goals and usually, the commercial ones come second (see Table 4.3). The analysis will test the fit of the specific expectations and goals of the Academy to the expectations and goals of the entire CR. It can be understood as a fit of a component within a system. The Academy, however, may choose to have a more general and un-quantified approach regarding the CR. This general strategy will determine a long-term approach towards CR projects, for example, a university may see its role in the development of a specific region, as its obligation to cooperate in CR with local industry.

---

[15]The term here also includes governmental and other non-profit research oriented organizations (for example, research institutes).

Table 4.3: Players' (Academy) Parameters[16]

Parameter	Positive	Negative
Clarity of CR goals		
Fit of CR goals and academy goals		
Importance of non commercial goals (high, low)		
Importance of commercial goals (high, low)		

Source: Author's own.

The non-commercial goals may however have some commercial aspects:

1. Ability to employ students, buy equipment, and perform the research; at university level and the research level.
2. Ability to reach research results and publish them.
3. Acquire means for support of collaboration with former students.
4. Connections with the industry, source for future research funding, consulting, and donations.

The commercial goals:

1. Financing on-going and future research.
2. Increasing and improving the research infrastructure.
3. Whenever possible, licensing the research results for royalties.

Industry

While for this player the basic interest is commercial, even if long-term, other interests can also exist and should be analyzed as part

---

[16] The table is presented as template, to be filled in by the user/reader.

of the model. The industry has a unique role, as it is expected to execute the results of the CR, and therefore, the fit expected from the CR and the industry regarding the end goal is extremely important. For the other players the ability of the Industry to utilize the CR results is very important (see Table 4.4). For the Government that ability is the basis for the economic growth expected from the CR. For the Academy, it is the basis for assuming that the CR will be utilized attaining both the strategic goals and the economic goals.

Table 4.4: Players' (Industry) Parameters[17]

Parameter	Positive	Negative
Clarity of CR goals		
Fit of CR goals and industry goals		
Importance of non-commercial goals (high, low)		
Sectorial unity of the industry involved (high, low)		

Source: Author's own.

Internationality of Players

A further complication in the matter is the impact that international players have on the projects. This dimension of the internationality of players can be analyzed on two plains. They are as follows:

1. The Legal Plain: Different nations having different legal systems influencing several important aspects—the ownership of the results; the protection and related issues of the IP; the rules regarding the allowed acts for each partner (owning subsidiary of different kinds and so on); the

---

[17]The table is presented as template to be filled in by the user/reader.

legal rights of the specific inventors; and the financial relations between the different parties, what constitutes an income, who is entitled or allowed to receive revenues and in what form.
2. The cultural differences, the way each country sees the internal relations in the different institutes, and how they manage and conduct things. This is the same problem encountered by multi-nationals trying to find a comprehensive system to manage operations in different countries. In fact, from this aspect the joint activity can be seen as a multi-national, with all the resulting problems.

With increasing globalization within industry and the already well-established globalization of sciences, it would seem that international differences, while not negligible are, however, at least of the same magnitude of the disciplinary differences. Thus, it would seem that for a pharmaceuticals firm to collaborate with a software house is difficult, due to the differences between sectors and their cultures, while the nationality is less important. It is not that national and, therefore, cultural differences stemming from that are non-existent, but for some firms the differences between the sectors are bigger than the national differences. However, it would seem that relational assets like learning to cooperate can be beneficial for both cases.

SUMMARY

This chapter introduced in detail the roles and interaction among the various partners in CR. As CR is a collaborative activity, it is necessary to understand the role of the participants in order to understand CR itself. The different roles of the Government, the Academy, and the Industry, as well as, parameters for their analysis were presented. IPR and other legal aspects were described briefly, and will be discussed in the following chapters in more detail. Also, the aspect of international and inter-sector cooperation was analyzed. The next chapter shall describe the partners in CR in great detail.

5

The Partners and their Roles

The first part of the book ends here. Being an introduction to the topic of CR it was naturally descriptive; focusing on describing the way things operate rather than on the optimal ways in which things should be done. The topics described in the first chapters—such as the roles of the different partners, the benefits each derive from CR, legal and IP issues—will also be discussed in the coming chapters. But the focus will remain on the way they should be handled, basing the recommendations on examples and practices.

The players are fundamental to understanding any system, and especially, one as complicated as CR. It is paramount to understand the role the players are expected to play in the system, as well as, predict how well they are going to perform it. It is important to analyze the hopes and fears of the players and how these may affect the fulfillment of each player's role in the system.

This chapter depicts the role of each type of player, also describing the interaction and conflicts between them. The drawings and examples are used to illustrate these roles and conflicts, and how these can hinder the effectiveness of CR. The external viewer would understand the importance of such an introduction, but it would appear that in some instances, even seasoned players are unaware of the reasons behind the behavior of their partners towards the CR projects, deeming them obstinate or conservative. It is hoped that now, the Industrial partners can better understand the Academy and the Academy understands their Industrial partners. The veteran partners can put this understanding into positive effect. The Industry should understand that the crucial role played by the publications cannot be overlooked. Similarly, the Academy should also understand that the industry's insistence on confidentiality has real reasons and its not mere paranoia. The results of the fears of Industry and the Academy in the by-laws of the SRJV's are also described and explained.

THE DUAL PERSPECTIVE

The dual perspective refers here to the inter-relations between pairs of players (see Figure 5.1 and Figure 5.2). The analysis refers to the dual relationships between the major players, as a prelude to analyzing the more complex inter-relationships among all the players (see Figure 5.1).

Figure 5.1: Government–Industry Interaction

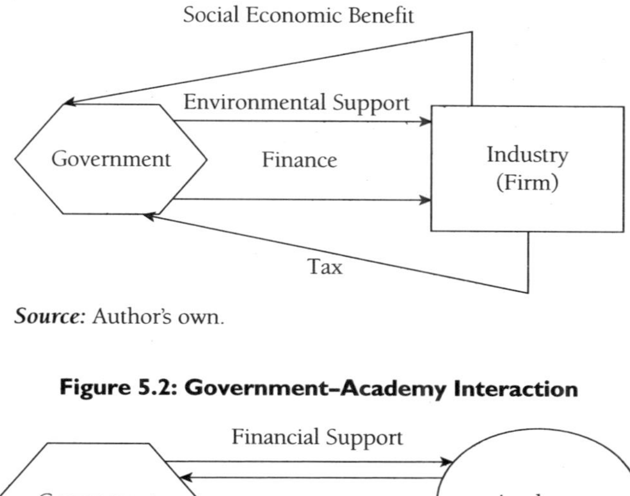

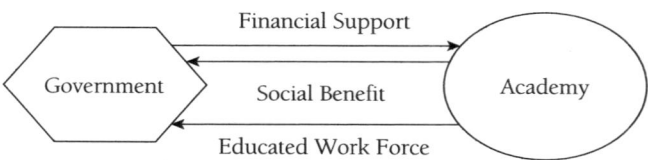

Source: Author's own.

Figure 5.2: Government–Academy Interaction

Source: Author's own.

The government supplies the firms with a working environment, economic conditions, monetary regulation, legal environment, labor and firm laws and so on. It also supplies funding directly via stipends, grants, and favored loans to encourage production, export and other goals. The firm in turn supplies the government with taxes, and with other social economic benefits, employment, purchases from suppliers and so on.

The government supplies the Academy with the working environment as it does to all, but it also supplies the academy with funding, at least at some level, for the public institutes. In turn, the academy supplies the government and the nation in general with a trained and efficient workforce. On an even more general level, the academy also supplies some social economic benefit to the society it operates via, social studies, humanities, medical research, training, and more. Now for a closer look at the partners.

INDUSTRY

Industrial research is not conducted for fun, or, without a specific target in mind, as the work is mostly for development. It is characterized by a compromise between performance and cost. The industry tries to get as much as possible for as less monetary investment as possible. While for the marketing department, issues such as positioning and competitive advantage seem important and crucial enough to dictate some of the characteristics of the desired products, that is not the case for development. Development being the last stage before production is mainly concerned with costs, and at best with cost and quality combined. The demand for reduced cost can drive development, while apparently not improving the product performance. The best way to describe such development work is in electrical engineering.

Box 5.1: Product Cost Reduction

A device is developed by a communications firm to allow the use of third-generation technology usage by second-generation, hand-held computers. That device is costly and its initial cost is around 1,000 US$. The product is then introduced into the market, and within 6 months has managed

Contd. Box 5.1

Contd. Box 5.1

> to obtain 25 percent of the market. The competition follows and similar devices appear in the market.
>
> The firm is facing a familiar phenomenon. It cannot continuously improve the device, as it has to be able to interact with the central systems providing the services and therefore, it is *imprisoned* by the third generation technology standards, and is not able to move incrementally towards higher performance. Its own performance is already limited by the supporting systems. The only way the product can evolve is by becoming more user friendly and accessible to the market. The engineers have a well-defined task, while keeping the scope of the feature fixed, within a defined range, they have to play with the composition of hardware and software, in order to reduce the cost of the product. Thus, costs can be reduced by more efficient manufacturing, reduced components costs, or a combination of the two. As work progresses, more commercially advanced and available components are introduced, economy of scale is incorporated wherever possible, and slowly the cost is reduced. The cost reduction has nothing to do with the market price reduction, which is a variable, dependent upon the competitiveness of the market, and some market characteristics. The reduction in market price is normally faster than the reduction in product cost, and therefore slowly erodes the profit margins of the product for the firm. However, long before the product becomes unprofitable, or close to that, a new technology (fourth generation) will supplement the entire product line and the process will start again.

The process described above describes the work performed by engineers so as to achieve well-defined and constrained goals, involving technology and costing. The research work done is more basic and more technological, but the issue of costs and alternative costs always appears in the background. A research example to fit the example above would be the development of a new design for a system for the next generation of communications.

Box 5.2: Next Generation R&D

> The R&D department has another section employing not only engineers but also applied research personnel. That section does more research-like work where it deals mostly with technology at its purest form. That section is basically interested in performance, and in defining the

Contd. Box 5.2

Contd. Box 5.2

> technology envelop that will define the next generation of the products. It will not deal directly with the cost of the products, but it will define their role and the entire system architecture. In the example mentioned above, the firm is trying to develop a line of products for beyond Third Generation of communication (3G). The basic technology definitions exist and define the interoperability of systems and components, their communication protocols, and their overall characteristics. However, the actual work of incorporation of the codes into software and the hardware into models for future products is still done individually by every player in the market. The section dealing with research in the firm is doing that. While keeping to the evolving standards it develops basic models, concept proving models and system architectures for the firm's products. These products will have to demonstrate that they have the features and capabilities within the limits set by the definitions of the standards for the fourth generation. It will later be the duty of the development section to make these into marketable, cost worthy products.

Even if originally the firm's research is not led entirely by the cost objectives, it is nonetheless influenced by it. Furthermore, it should be remembered that the firms perform the research for commercial purposes, and will do so only towards defined and seemingly logical ends.

The only exception to the definitions and description above is the large firms. These organizations do deal from time to time with basic, scientific-like research without an attainable purpose in the future. Firms do not deal with basic high-risk research for their own sake. However, they would engage in such research only because they deem the technological potential of the results to be of high strategic importance in the long-term for them. High strategic importance means that it can be translated into a commercial advantage, even if initially when first embarked upon, its commercial advantage is not quantifiable.

R&D BENEFITS

The benefits of development of new products, especially in the high-technology world are well-known and appreciated. The simplest to understand is the development of a new drug. It is well-known that a firm can benefit and make billions in revenues, if it is able to patent a drug, and later receive the FDA or EC approval for use. However, the involvement of firms in Applied Research, in the basic development of technologies is more complex to understand. Do firms involved in the Applied Research (Generic Research, as sometimes it is called), reap any benefits from that activity? After all, generic technologies can be licensed. Sometimes they are introduced as standards and made available for free. The qualitative explanations, regarding the ownership of the technology are well-known and deal with the advantage of experience and familiarity with the new technology, the edge of being first in the market, being innovative and therefore more competitive. However, the crucial question is: Are there also any known economic benefits?

In his thesis, Amiram Porath (Porath, 2007, 2008b) shows that firms involved in generic R&D in consortia with the Academy in all sectors, perform better economically during times of crises, than similar firms in the same markets and with similar other parameters. The assumption that "**Firm Income is higher for firms that invest in generic R&D than for firms that do not invest in generic R&D**", deals with the benefit that firms performing generic R&D derive from that activity. Firms are economic organizations whose main direct economic activity is revenue generation. While generic R&D may not be obviously and directly linked to revenue generation in a certain year, it was expected that generic R&D would have some effect on revenue (preferred definition over income), otherwise firms would not perform generic R&D. The link between economic benefits and generic R&D was at best considered weak. From the data summarized in the research mentioned, it would appear that the firms in the sampled population were, in normal years (for example, preceding the crises years) not divided significantly into generic R&D performers and non-generic R&D performers in regular years. However, in economic crisis years, 2001–2003, the group bifurcated into two significant groups. One must note that the research left one major point for future research and that is the causality:

Do firms that perform better in the market also elect to perform generic R&D, or is it that because the firm performs generic R&D that it performs better? It may be considered that the performance of generic R&D as it involves long-term planning and better than average understanding of the market that the activity itself is beneficial, but that would require further substantiation. At least for investors the causality is less important when selecting investment opportunities.

Thus, the work showed that generic R&D could be regarded as a strategic activity with clear benefits for the performance and even survival of the firm. The research (Porath, 2007, 2008a) was based on analysis of the performance of the two groups of firms, in two different periods. The economic crisis years were characterized by CBS (2003) as a change in the national GDP, growth market by the leading industrial sector of electronics, for the Israeli economy. The slow-down in the economy during 2001 to 2003 was correlated (with a small delay) with the significant difference in the income trend (positive) for firms dealing with generic R&D, compared to the other firms in same sectors (negative trend) not dealing with generic R&D (but dealing with R&D in general).

INDUSTRY SCALE OF VALUES

The ability to perform industrial research while obtaining in the fastest possible way the characteristics required, or reaching the cost goals in the fastest way, are the basis for evaluation in that world. A good engineer solving costing problems and being able to combine low cost components with improved production techniques is much favored. Such performance is encouraged by commercial incentives, promotion and other means.

INDUSTRY FEARS

The main point of worry for a firm entering a CR is the spillover of the knowledge (Audretsch and Feldman, 1996; Kaiser, 2002b;

Kamien et al., 1992; Katsoulacos and Ulph, 1998; Miyagiwa and Ohno, 2002). The economic aspect of participation and the required investment is second in importance. Most firms in R&D intensive sectors are accustomed to high investments in R&D and the CR financial support is normally under better conditions, than the firms can get elsewhere. The reason for joining CR is the wish to gain strategic advantage based upon a technological edge. There is an added strategic value in gaining partnership and learning to combine forces and cooperate with other players in the market, but that is, deemed less direct (see Chapter 9).

Spillovers

Spillovers have the ability to render all the research effort empty. We shall define spillover *as an unintended transfer of knowledge from one entity to another*. They can take place in several forms:

1. Through knowledge transfer via the transfer of personnel.
2. Through presentations and publications.
3. Through efforts by the receiving party such as reverse engineering, interviews, etc.
4. Through the cooperative effort in joint research projects.

Some writers (Katsoulacos and Ulph, 1998; Kamien et al., 1992) regard the spillover as an exogenous effect derived from every day events in the sector-rate of personnel exchange between firms and similar events. Another point of view (Katsoulacos and Ulph, 1998), regards the phenomenon as endogenous; derived from the close cooperation between the partners. The competitive edge is lost by spillovers, while the developing cost is still incurred. The level of risk for spillovers is different from one sector to another, and is influenced by characteristics of the sector, such as, the level of IPR protection, and the rate of personnel exchange. In sectors such as pharmaceuticals, where the IPR protection is high, the risk from spillovers is low. In sectors with lower IPR protection efficiency, such as, software, where the personnel exchange is also very high rate, the risk of spillovers is very high.

Box 5.3: Spillover

Several firms join forces in an effort to develop applications for next generation of Telecom products. The firms do not limit their joint effort to the development of technologies and prototypes for applications, but also to promote through standardization bodies, standards that would support their products and applications. The rate of personnel movement in the sector is high, and although not all exchange occurs between partners in the consortium, some cases are the same. A year after the joint work ends, some firms find themselves with competing products in the market, competing with their former partners. Even if the algorithms can be protected for the applications, it is very difficult to show through the small differences, that these actually are not the same products, and to delineate a clear border between the specific and private applications developed by specific firms, and the compliance with the jointly promoted standards.

Box 5.4: IP Limitations

Firms researching breast cancer in a joint project develop encapsulating technologies and try them on drug candidates owned by some of the partners. At the end of the project, with the potential spillover, the strict patenting and enforcement of the IPR do not allow the utilization of the knowledge by partners, not owning the IP. The exchange rate of personnel is low and not often between partners, but the patents do not allow the use of patented molecules by non-owners or licensees, and the encapsulation technologies again are limited by specificity.

CR Worries

The experienced firms in CR, by nature of the CR are less worried from spillovers to their CR partners. There are several reasons for that; first is that the partners are selected, and if a firm is worried ex-ante from spillover to any partner it will either try and block that partner from joining or it will exit itself; the second reason is that each of the members puts itself at risk by donating something into the general pool, and each partner has an interest to make sure that the others' contribution is important to them. Thus, a balance of terror of sorts is created within the CR. The big worry is the spillover of information to external entities. These entities are not part of the Balance of Terror, and do not even participate in the costs of the research to create the knowledge they may get. They therefore have a strong incentive to try and get the knowledge. Therefore, the CR participants will try and lower the spillover risk as far as possible (see Figure 5.3), blocking the entry of firms with low potential for the Balance of Terror.

Figure 5.3: The Spillover Conflict

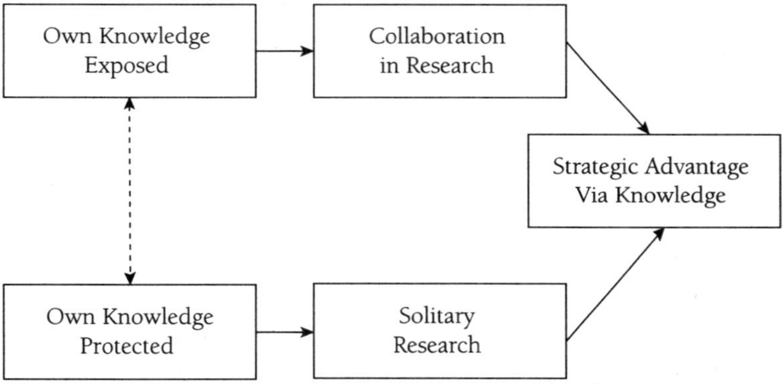

```
┌──────────────┐      ┌──────────────┐
│ Own Knowledge│─────▶│ Collaboration│
│   Exposed    │      │  in Research │
└──────────────┘      └──────────────┘
       ▲                      │
       ┆                      ▼
       ┆              ┌──────────────┐
       ┆              │   Strategic  │
       ┆              │   Advantage  │
       ┆              │ Via Knowledge│
       ┆              └──────────────┘
       ▼                      ▲
┌──────────────┐      ┌──────────────┐
│ Own Knowledge│─────▶│   Solitary   │
│  Protected   │      │   Research   │
└──────────────┘      └──────────────┘
```

Source: Author's own.

The second big worry regarding spillovers, is with respect to the Academy. The same characteristics that make the Academy such a good research partner in basic research—the openness, the free access to external knowledge—also make it a huge risk, when the knowledge source is within the CR, and not external to it. Here, it is important to understand the role of publications in the academic world.[18]

The conflict cannot be compromised. However, it could be broken by finding the correct combination of the entities, the knowledge

---

[18]For example, Israeli universities do not allow in their by-laws the approval of a confidential thesis for MS or PhD, as publication is the only viable way to estimate the level of the research. As most research in these universities is done by students guided by faculty members, it is impossible to have confidential research done in the Israeli academy ex-ante.

is exposed to (for example, non-competing ones) and limiting its transfer to potentially dangerous or unknown entities. The following sections will provide an explanation for how this is done.

Results in CR

In the SRJVs, we will find in the by-laws the signs of the attempts to lower the spillover risks, which will be expressed in several ways, some of which are:

1. Limitation on publication/transfer of non-self knowledge without the permission of the knowledge owner.
2. Screening and approval processes for publications (depending on the involvement and the power of the academy involved these measures will be up to censorships of publication or as weak as to require just notification).
3. Ethical regulation regarding personnel recruiting from partners in the project.
4. Limitations on the transfer of the partnership in the projects to affiliates and requirements regarding change of ownership and Mergers with other players in the market.
5. Requirements to protect IPR, or allowing another member to do so.

ACADEMY POINT OF VIEW

The Academy is interested in education and in the creation of knowledge. These can be seen as two facets of the same process. One is the creation of knowledge, that is, new to the world, which we call research, and the second, the creation of that knowledge which may not be new to the world, in new minds. The education aspect has little to do with the research and the development, except in the provision of an assistive workforce for the principal researchers, the research students.

Academic research, at its purest form is aimed at increasing the understanding of newly observed phenomena, and the solving of long standing problems. It is not aimed for commercial ends and has no direct links to market issues. It can be linked however to the outside life, especially when solving such external problems for the general benefit of the community. The academy believes that, only the sharing of ideas and the continual mutual fertilization can assure the progress of science, and the creation of new ideas and better understanding. The academic community therefore assumes that knowledge has to be shared in order for it to grow. That, in time, it will lead to some basic behavior patterns characteristic of academic work environment:

> **Box 5.5: Academic Performance Evaluation**
>
> In an engineering department in a leading university, two new candidates are undergoing evaluation for acceptance into the department. Both have good grades in their studies and in their thesis for PhD; however they differ in their post-doc work. Candidate A has very good records of problem solving in engineering and in designing of new technical models. Most of his articles are published in trade magazines, and show good understanding of technical problems, and a good ability of solving them. "A" has managed to secure some High-Tech industrial grants of significant size for his labs. Candidate B is different, he has published a smaller number of articles, mostly in very prestigious scientific journals that have been widely read and cited in subsequent articles by other researchers. "B" has been invited to present a paper, and write articles by the leading scientific journals in the field. "B" has, however, managed to get only a small academic research grant, and has few, if any, contacts within the industry, as the research topics dealt with by "B" are far from application, and therefore of little importance for the industry. Which will the department prefer? In normal academic environment, "B" will be preferred over "A". "A" probably could find a good position in a research institute or the industry.

The importance of publishing to the academic world has been mentioned several times, and we will go into it when discussing the conflict description. However, it is important to mention here, as well as in other places, that publication is not a just a fad of the academic world, it serves two purposes:

1. Dissemination of the knowledge to the academic community, thus ensuring the further growth of the knowledge.
2. A measuring tool for the quality of the research performed by the single researcher or the team.

Applied Research

The academic outlook at applied research is complex. The increase in finance for applied research from various resources makes that sort of research very attractive to technologically oriented research topics. In such areas, research is very expensive and therefore tends to follow finance sources. However, in the academic world, such research has a reputation as being low level and secondary. It is harder to publish applied research results in leading magazines, and it can often be unpublishable at all.

Research has shown that applied research does not reduce the overall basic research performed by academic researchers. It does show, however, a tendency to reduce the amount of basic, long-term research, the older the researcher gets (Kyvik and Olsen, 2008). The young researchers tend to invest more in basic research in order to base their academic status, and to create the basis for applied research. As researchers aged, the applied research ratio of their overall research increased. The older researchers require fewer acceptances by the academic world, attained by basic research work, and therefore tend to increase their applied work. They also need less basic research to establish their own proprietary knowledge base. That would imply that short-term research can, and is, performed more by the advanced (age-wise) researchers. However, it would seem that for researchers starting young, applied research and its enhanced financing opportunities holds more in store than for the better established researchers. The starting researcher, needing to build a lab and a team would find applied research very appealing. However, it is wrong to look at researchers as performing one kind of research or another. Due to the nature of research funding, and the fact that funding sources requires preparation time and incurs delays from the publication of call to the commencement of the project—add to that the uncertainty of success of a proposal for research—researchers normally find that at times they may have more than one project or, none at all. The variation in the research burden requires that the researcher also diversify the research resources, and therefore also the research type. It is more appropriate to discuss research diversity as a *researcher's portfolio*. It would therefore be natural[19] to expect to find in a researcher's portfolio both basic and applied research. In fact, the Fraunhoffer system is based on the assumption that such a portfolio not only exists, but also has a synergetic effect. The support for basic research is increased correspondingly to the amount of cooperation with the industry (including applied research).

PARTNER ROLES

The different partners will have different roles in Collaborative Research. The Industry will need to bear in mind and constantly maintain the joint effort focused on a specific predetermined goal, in order to assure the potential of attaining this goal. The Academy will have a more innovative role in trying unorthodox ways for attaining the goal. The roles can be analyzed sequentially or through a parallel view. The parallel view will see both partners working jointly at the same time doing two different and complementary roles. The sequential view will see the sort of cooperation seen in relay racing. As in relay racing when the first runner passes the baton to the next one, both are working to assure a swift and secure passage. But during the other parts of the race, each runner is working on his own to do the best he can, during the time he is holding the baton, and trusting the others to perform well when it is their turn.

---

[19]This discussion relates to research systems in which the researcher is not fully financed via a central, national or regional source.

The Sequential View

When observed, knowledge creation seems to have a sequential or evolutionary character (see Figure 5.4), passing from basic research to applied research; and from there through knowledge protection to the licensing and the later development stages, leading from basic knowledge to a marketable product or process. Under that view, the cooperation between Academy and Industry is seen, as if, the process is divided into responsibility domains, dominated in turn by each partner. Such was the view of the EU commission regarding Framework Program 5 projects. The first stages would be of basic research dominated by the Academy, with the Industry passing general information, and mostly being kept in *the know*, but not contributing much to the research itself. After that stage, the applied research would commence with the industry, leading the definitions and characterization of the technology and the architecture of the systems. It also has a more dominant role in the actual research work being performed; and up to initial product development, totally controlled by the industry and performed almost entirely by it, with a small contribution from the Academy. The research baton is passed during the applied research phase when both sides are working together (running together); the Industry picking up speed and the Academy slowing down. As in the race example, each partner is interested in the progress made by its partner and attempts to be informed on progress and give additional input whenever possible. This is true cooperation.

Figure 5.4: Sequential View

Source: Author's own.

The Parallel View

In the parallel view, both partners are working together on different tasks at the same time and the division of the tasks is done according to the characteristics of the tasks—the partners are both working and keep being informed on the other partner's progress at the same time (see Figure 5.5). The Magnet consortia are a good example of that view:

Box 5.6: Magnet 2

In the Magnet consortia for communications, the Industry and the Academy work simultaneously, trying to solve research problems and perform applied research to develop technology platforms. The Industry defines the needs and performance level expected from the desired research products and the Academy takes the specific problems that are of a more basic nature, developing general concepts and technologies that fit into the applied research performed by the industry. Both partners work together simultaneously and keep each other informed of their progress; to learn of breakthroughs and to make sure they would still converge at the end and not disperse too much. The industry will try to define the joint platform to be developed and to assure that it would fit with the emerging standards for that specific generation of future products. The academy at the same time will try and solve some of the coding problems, as well as, the basic architectures that could fit the specifications given by the industry but which seem to be insurmountable by current technological standards.

Figure 5.5: Parallel View

Academy Industry Basic Research According to Basic Demands	→	Academy Industry Further Validation of Knowledge to Fit Standards	→	Academy Industry Further Development

Source: Author's own.

As can be seen from this illustration, both possibilities exist in programs for CR, and for certain, will also exist without a structured program. It can be further claimed, that in real life, both possibilities exist at the same time, in the same project, although normally only one would be dominant. That is to say, that in a large project with numerous sub-tasks, some would be done in parallel and some in sequence, but one mode of operation will be dominant. Therefore, when claiming that both Academy and Industry participate in a project, it is not very easy to answer which mode will they prefer and which role will they assume?

The answer partly lies with the environment in which the project is operating. When the project is operating in a structured environment, then the funding authority will define the character of the research, thereby defining the partner responsible for performance, and the preferred mode. When the scene is not structured, normally the funding source will assume the defining role.

The Industry will normally wish to work sequentially, where not so much supervision is required; the Academy is given a set of characterization, specifications and some constraints, and is required to give an answer, which the Industry can take and use as it likes without too much interference from the Academy. Confidentiality is another matter to be considered. The sequential mode reduces the risk of spillover from academic research, regarding development data. Even if the basic research results leak, they are still removed enough from the development data to prevent real damage. However, for the Academy, it is normally better to be involved in the entire process, best done via the parallel mode, and thus maintaining close control over the usage its knowledge is put to. The Academy would normally license the knowledge it has developed, and the revenues would depend on the utilization of that knowledge, which is another incentive for the Academy to be involved throughout the project life.

Thus, the Industry would normally supply the performance requirements and the artificial constraints resulting from marketing demands. The Academy will supply the basic knowledge, which would need further development in order to become useful. The structured programs would normally give more power to the industry for two reasons:

1. Industry seems to be better equipped for project management from the administrative point of view.
2. Industry is better equipped to make sure the knowledge developed is put to use in the future.

Since most structured programs are required to show that they are well managed, and that the public funds invested are utilized efficiently, it further increases the industrial fit for the role of project leader, according to reason 1. Since these programs are also established to assure some beneficial impact, the utilization partner is normally given preference in goal definition and in management: reason 2. Reason 2 can be further clarified by stating, that in order for the knowledge to be utilized, it has to be in the right format, fit the relevant standards, and comply with the relevant economic considerations. All these aspects are more within the industrial purview than the academic research culture. But there also might be a possibility that, technically sound, academically developed knowledge may be un-usable for the industry due to lack of economic considerations, or standards fit.

SUMMARY

This chapter closes the first part of the book. This part dealt with the description and explanation of CR, the role of the partners and the benefits that are supposed to come out of it. Therefore, it was very descriptive and did not refer to the optimal way of doing things nor gave an opinion which way is better. The first part is intended for understanding CR as it is and the roles of the different players as they see it. In this chapter, the roles of the partners and their wishes and fears were described. The different paths, the parallel and the sequential views were also described. It is known from long experience that the differences and the positions of the partners are not as well understood as could be desired, and hopefully this chapter would have helped clear this up. It is very confusing sometime for the partners to understand each other, and their obstinacy regarding certain points (publishing, for example, is often the main problem; the Industry just cannot believe that the Academy does not see the risk, and the Academy does not understand how the Industry cannot understand that the Academy "must" publish), is the source of many conflicts. The results of the fears of the industry and the academy in the by-laws of the SRJVs have also been described and explained.

Earlier chapters have dealt with other aspects of the CR, the need for it, and other different options regarding R&D. They also include the introduction of the applied research and its role in academic research compared to basic research within the researcher's portfolio; the role of the applied research and its potential for young and old researchers. The next section of the book will be more practically oriented and will deal with questions like: What to do with CR options? How to create CR options to fit the needs of the different players? What should each player ask of the others? And what to do when one is left outside an SRJV?

Part II

Practical Aspects

6

When should You get into a Collaborative Project?

This chapter describes the rationale behind the decision to enter, or not enter the project. I will present some of the economic research analyzing the influence of such projects on an industry, and will show in which industries and cases the firms will have to make every possible effort to get in and when they will be able to forgo such participation. In order to better understand the decision making process and considerations, a model is presented regarding the formation process of SRJV. Since the decision to establish Collaborative Research is of a strategic nature and is not only involving significant budgetary issues, but dealing with core issues in technological sectors—knowledge and development—it has to be treated as part of the specific firm strategy. This chapter discusses the decision process and different strategic parameters are identified and discussed. The importance of the sector and its characteristics are discussed (concentration, other consortia and so on). Once such a step has been taken, the firm needs to follow through, or according to pre-established milestones, decide to withdraw. "How to live inside a Collaborative Research Project" will be discussed elsewhere.

Economic research using mathematically developed models has shown that collaborative research in certain formulae is socially beneficial both to the firms involved and to society in general (Kamien et al., 1992). The benefit to society is derived by reducing the development costs and thus the cost to the final consumers.

Economic research however has shown several dangers regarding such cooperation. Originally, the greatest fear from collaborative research is that of collusion. That fear has long delayed the legal approval for R&D consortia, until the early 1980's, both in the US and EU (Miyagiwa and Ohno, 2002). That limitation was not relevant to the Academy–Industry cooperation; as such cooperation was not deemed to be liable for collusion. McKelvey (1997), later supported by Vonortas (2002), stipulates that a firm's strategic intent is driven by changes in the institutional and competitive environment. The fact that changes in the environment affect firms in similar ways, it results in those firms defining problems also in a similar manner (Ahuja, 2000). Parkhe (1993), stated that higher the expectations for the future, the more shadowy that future is. Understanding the environment will have an influence on a firm's strategy (Barr, Stimpert, and Huff, 1992; Teece, 1996). These points regarding similarity and expectations are important for understanding the model developed for this research on which it is based. The behavioral and organization effects of the increased closeness between Industry and Academy on the culture of the Academy, and the priorities of the researchers in the academy has interested researchers (Brooks and Randazzese, 1998; Etzkowitz, 1999; Siegel et al., 1999; Slaughter and Leslie, 1997; Van Geehuizen, 1997) Some of the discussion has focused on the Technology Transfer methods. It is accepted that there are several mechanisms: Teaching, Research Students, Consulting, and Joint projects. The Technology Transfer Office/Company (TTO/TTC) is a facilitator of the last activities, and serves also to help the researchers formulate and protect their Knowledge, (Parker and Zilberman, 1993). The role of the TTO and TTC has become more and more professional, trying to develop guidelines and rules for joint action (Rogers et al., 2000). The AUTM in the USA and ProTon Europe (as well as other such as EARTO, EUA, and more) in the EU have also become professional associations.

The discussion of Academy–Industry cooperation in the USA cannot be done without mention of the Bayh–Dole Act in 1980. This Act allowed universities to register patents assigned to them resulting from publicly funded research, and enjoy the proceeds.

That law had a significant influence on the activity in the Academy and the way applied research was viewed, both by the researchers and by the management in the Academy (Mowery et al., 1999). Since the US Act of 1984, and the launching of the EU research Framework Programs in 1985, the cooperation even on Industry–Industry level was given legal legitimacy. The analysis will deal specifically with the Academy–Industry cooperation, leaving out the Industry–Industry cooperation aspect.

FORMATIVE PROCESS

The formation process of CR is extremely important for the analysis of the participation and the decision involved. The background research regarding the formation of RJV is analyzed, as the preview for understanding the formation process and its parameters.

General Relevance

The creation of a new organizational form is not hard to demonstrate in the case of the Magnet Program, as there are ample signs of it (Porath, 2008b). However, it is necessary to understand some of the assumptions regarding its structure and environment as part of the basis for the proposed model. As mentioned above, McKelvey (1997), later supported by Vonortas (2002), stipulates that a firm's strategic intent is driven by changes in the institutional and competitive environment. The fact that changes in the environment will affect the firms in it in similar ways, results in those firms defining problems similarly (Ahuja, 2000). The environment has an influence on the strategic intent of the firm, as well as, on the definition of their problem. Here, we are interested in the effect the environment will have on the way firms develop administrative mechanisms and formal structures, as a result of its future expectations, which are derived from their perception of the environment. Higher the expectations for the future, the more shadowy that future is, and hence, greater the necessity for formal safeguards (Parkhe, 1993). These points regarding similarity and expectations are important for understanding the DOR model upon which the model developed for this research is based. In direct relevance to our model, Barr, Stimpert, and Huff (1992) elaborated on the cognitive aspects of the link between the manager's understanding of environmental conditions and a firm's strategy, which they perceived to be a critical one. Teece (1996) deals with the link to the industry, as a drive to affect strategy, and introduces the idea that formal as well as informal structures prevalent in the industry, combined with the links the firm has, will determine the options open to the firm, leading to a limited range of action options available. Teece (1996) also mentions the characteristics of technological development and the environmental and technological uncertainty involved. Sanchez and Mahoney (1996) couple the organizational structure to effective coordination and performance, introducing modularity to the general design.

Relevant Empirical Research

The next section will describe some of the empirical work done so far. The empirical work will be described first in relation to the focused theories mentioned before, and in the last part with a more strategic view, regarding generalized models. This section lays the foundation for the gaps in the research (theory and empirical work) to be addressed by the model and the hypotheses later on.

Focused Research

Empirical research relevant to the topic of RJV and their structure can be found in only a small number of works (Kaiser, 2002b; Luukkonen, 1998, 2000), mainly due to the dearth of large enough samples for such a study and the problem of statistical significance that this entails. Although limited, the experience described here is very positive and therefore encouraging; however, it would seem that further empirical work is necessary to lend credibility to the models. While Kaiser (2002b) focused on validating economic models for RJV relating to service sector firms in Germany, the Luukkonen research (1998, 2000) centered on an analysis of the EU Framework Programs and Eureka, in the context of their role in the R&D process and that of governments in supporting research. Tao and Wu (1997) may also be noted as an empirical study; in that it analyzes field data of R&D consortia reported by the *Wall Street Journal* between 1985 and 1992. Thus, we can see that the empirical work done so far has been limited both geographically and topic-wise. With regard to topics, it has been mostly restricted to a single discipline, and intended to prove a practical point. A review of the multi-disciplinary research and a fuller look at the RJV from its inception will be discussed in the following sections.

Broad Research

The research is termed "broad", as it brings together several disciplines into a general picture. I will describe the model presented by Doz, Olk, and Ring (2000), and after explaining the specific situation the model refers to—the RJV—will move to explain the SP model, which is the basis of my PhD research.

Extensive research, including case studies and general surveys, has been done regarding Academy–Industry cooperation. Still few analyses focus on R&D projects (Fontana et al., 2006), and less on the multi-partner generic R&D activities. Of the little multi-disciplinary empirical research that has been done on RJVs, the most pertinent is that of Doz, Olk, and Ring (2000). As the first comprehensive model to explore the links from initial conditions through formation and performance, to the follow-up into future R&D consortia, it is taken as a provisional template of the SP model. The model is based on the PhD dissertation of Peter Olk (1991), who collected empirical data on voluntary RJVs in the US, between 1984 and 1990, using half the data to formulate his model and half to validate it. Olk (1991) researched RJV projects registered in the US under the revised Antitrust Act of 1984, up to 1990. These RJV projects formed voluntarily by members, were not supported by the government directly, and had no pre-determined structure. They were registered under the act only to avoid charges of collusion under US law. The business environment in which the RJV projects were formed, therefore, influenced the model resulting from the data collected. The Dor, Olk, and Ring (DOR) model describes the environmental conditions that lead to the formation of an RJV, dictating the path of its formation, whether emergent or engineered, whether a Triggering Entity is used or not and, its resultant structure and performance. The performance combined with the results and the expectations of the participants then leads to an analysis of potential continuation (future RJV projects). The model utilizes the following stages: Environment, Formation, Performance, and Continuation.

Environment

Based on earlier literature mentioned in the previous two sections (McKelvey, 1997), the DOR model stipulates that the firm's strategic intent is driven by changes in its institutional and competitive environment, which affects all the firms in the environment in similar ways, such that they will define problems similarly (Ahuja, 2000). The DOR model does not relate to the specific reasons that lead firms to choose the RJV option. There is a parameter missing which would explain the preference for this course over others, such as commercial unification, the establishment of an association to lobby for political aid (including government support), and standardization. When dealing with SRJV, generic R&D is introduced as the missing parameter and preferred solution. DOR demonstrated that, the closer the common interests of the members of R&D consortia, the more they try to achieve a similar direction in their relationship. The DOR model predicts that the network is strong but the central component is weak, and members thus view the consortium as an option for working together based on their mutual interests, without the formal structure of the consortium.

Formation

There are two alternative paths described in the DOR model, an Emergent Process, which deals with formation of RJV projects voluntarily via the realization of a need to join forces, and an Engineered Process. The Engineered Process is a formation process enabled by a Triggering Entity: a person or a company that causes the parties of the future RJV to realize their need to come together, and thus triggers the formation of the RJV. The Triggering Entity normally operates when there are no recognized common threats/interests. A Triggering Entity is therefore required for formation, to a large extent determining membership and the formation process itself.

In the DOR model, a Triggering Entity is required to coordinate the recruiting activity, select potential members, and make them recognize the need to coordinate their activities, sometimes using strong pressure (Dyer and Nobeoka, 2000; Olk, 1991). The Triggering Entity becomes the center of the activity, sometimes the only contact between the partners. It works according to the structural holes in the network function described by Barr, Stimpert, and Huff (1992). Thus, in the early stages, when the firms are disconnected, the Triggering Entity controls the flow of information between them and can reveal opportunities created by changes in the environment. Considering its importance in selecting potential members and the centrality of its context, the Triggering Entity could also be an organization.

Performance

Since the DOR model assumes that the formation is voluntary and is based mostly on economics, it views the RJV from an economic viewpoint. The transaction costs of managing a large Engineered Process consortium will be increasingly larger, unless some mechanism for organizational learning appears to reduce them.

The networks will have to develop some inter-organizational learning, which will reduce the transaction cost, and also require some relational investment, leading to activities characteristic of the Emergent Process. An Emergent Process, on the other hand, will need to gravitate towards the innovation-promoting structure of the Engineered Process in order to respond to changing environmental conditions (Uzzi, 1997).

Continuation

As one might expect, cooperation will lead to ties between formerly estranged firms. While in an Emergent Process, firms are likely to be from the same industry or closely related in terms of goals and activities; this is not so for an Engineered Process, where firms are normally selected more for compatibility, and where close interaction may lead to improved connections (Doz, 1996; Gulati, 1995; Ring and Van de Ven, 1994). The results of the different processes will also mean that Emergent Process consortia, unlike Engineered Process consortia, are likely to encounter, fairly early, conflicts of interest, which may shorten their lives. However, this parameter deals with the post consortium activity and can be seen as the result of relational assets creation, done during the project lifetime.

Theoretical Background Summary

The literature surveyed shows the following gaps in the knowledge:

1. The DOR model analyzes (see Figure 6.1) only the voluntary duo cooperation Industry–Industry.
2. Empirical evidence is required for further substantiation not only of the full models but also for the partial economic models developed since the 1980s.
3. The role and benefit of the Generic R&D performed in the RJV/SRJV for the participating firms needs to be further empirically substantiated (Porath, 2007).

Figure 6.1: DOR Model

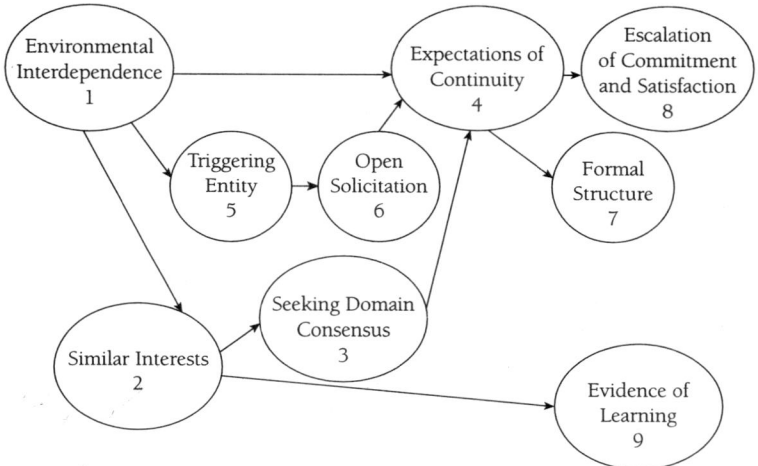

Source: Adaptation of the model based on Doz, Olk, and Ring (2000).

THE STRUCTURED PROGRAM (SP) MODEL

The DOR model dealt with firms forming alliances for joint R&D in the free market. The firms join forces in order to deal with threats or to exploit opportunities. In order to stay within the limits of the law, the firms elect to join forces in R&D, and do so without outside financial support. Since the early 1980s, regional, national, and supra-national governments have realized that in order to assist local economic development in the areas under their responsibility, they should support R&D and firms dealing with R&D. Thus, emerged Structured Research Joint Ventures (SRJV). SRJV are created in an environment very different from that of the DOR model. The firms in SRJV expect to be financially supported by the relevant authority. The support requires the authority involved to issue procedures for the proposal of an SRJV, the approval process (evaluation and awarding), monitoring (during the SRJV life time), post-SRJV evaluation of the results, and impact of the activity. Governmental accountability and public control have an impact on the SRJV environment, but will not be discussed here. Public funding, whether a grant or a loan, requires fairness and maintenance of competitive fairness. Therefore, most SRJV programs require that the firms deal within the SRJV for precompetitive research. Pre-competitive research is very difficult to measure, by definition, as it is more exclusive than inclusive. The simple solution to the measurement problem is to include a noncompetitive element—the academia research institutes (including university and research institutes). Thus, we have one more factor missing from the general DOR model, that is, the involvement of academia. The DOR model, being the first and most comprehensive model describing the formation and operational stages of a research consortium—created on the basis of data of free-forming R&D consortia in the USA—describes activities in a certain context. Most structured programs create SRJVs that are different and therefore cannot use the DOR model. In fact, the DOR model has relevance only to a very specific set of circumstances, and primarily in broad concept, and general parameters. In all SRJV programs, the program dictates the general structure of the consortia (legal framework), thus determining the basic level of the formal structure and the Intellectual Property rules (Porath, 2004, 2006).

Parameters of the SP Model

The proposed model (see Figure 6.2) includes some of the basic parameters of the DOR model. The SP model refers to the formation and pre-formation stages of the SRJV. The rationale behind this focus is two-fold. The first is that, once the consortium is formed, the program and its rules will dictate the rest—routines, internal organs, and so on—at least up to the point where there is little chance of differentiating between the characteristics of the specific consortium and the program itself. The second is that, in SRJV, the program will see formation of the consortium as a second level goal by itself—having projects that will hopefully do what the program wanted to have done. The basic assumption

Figure 6.2: The Structured Program (SP) Model

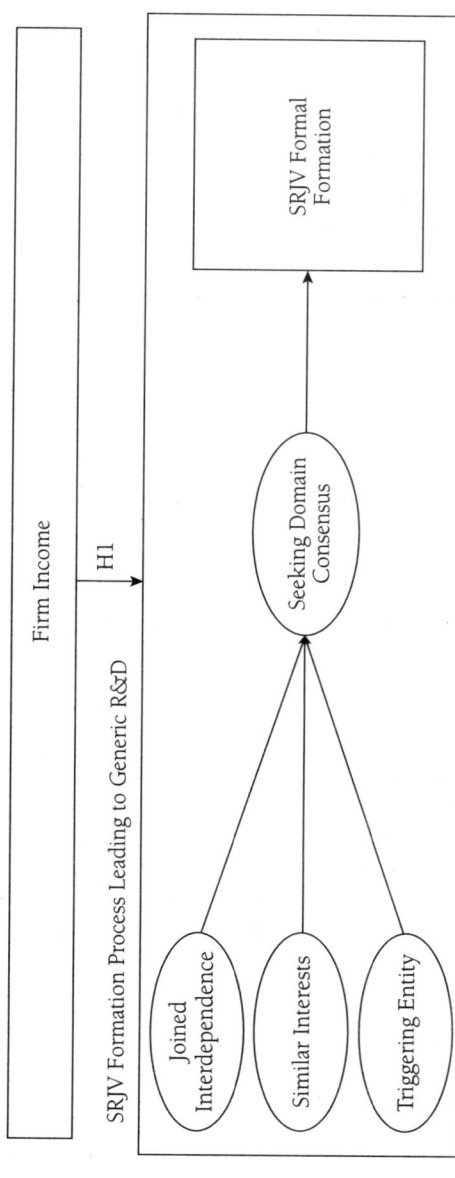

Source: (Porath, 2008a).

underlying the SP model is that generic R&D is beneficial for the firms involved. Without that assumption, the firms would not deal with that kind of activity. As economic development is the basis for most SRJV programs, that assumption is necessary for any model attempting to explain the SRJV programs. The benefit derived has to be economic for the assumption to have relevance. The next parameters will regard the early stages leading to the domain consensus.

Firm Income

It refers to the will, interest, and need to increase the income, which drives firms to consider the SRJV as a solution to their problems in the first place.

Joint Interdependence

It is that *fatal* link between the potential partners that will lead them to understand that they need to come together for the benefit of all. Therefore, joint interdependence will mean for us dependence of the firms on each other for performance and even their survival. The performance and survival of one will affect the others. They need not necessarily all be in the same sector or only in that sector, but they will have dependence. Since the joint interdependence can arise from numerous reasons, the realization of it can also occur at different points. For the purposes of this research in this parameter, the point of realization is not important. It is just important that at some point in the past, the firms have realized this and have decided to try and come together. This realization is measured by the past behavior of the firms.

Similar Interests

This is shared by players in the same or very closely related sectors. These players do not necessarily play similar roles. Suppliers, manufacturers, integrators, consultants, and others may share similar interests, even if they (due to the variety of roles and diversity of business) do not share joint interdependence. Similar Interests would mean that the firms are active in the same sector and would like to see it develop and evolve further. It is measured as a parameter dealing with the characteristics of the sector. These characteristics will hinder or assist the realization of the firms that they have to come together for their own benefit. Firms and other players, including academia, normally dependant on the sector, would come together in different ways.

Triggering Entity[20]

This is the third parameter, and it is linked to the Engineered Process in the DOR model. When the firms fail to realize Joint Interdependence or Similar Interests (or sometimes even when they do realize those) and the firms fail to overcome obstacles in coming together, such an entity may play the role of bringing them together. The existence of a Triggering Entity normally signifies a closed or non-open process of joining. In this specific research, the role of the Triggering Entity will mostly be limited to the stages leading to the Kick-Off meeting and thus to the Domain Consensus. In the DOR model, it has a bigger role also influencing the format of the specific RJV project and playing a significant role in its performance. In the SRJV, the structured nature of the SRJV projects is formed and their management routines would not allow for such a role to be played by the Triggering Entity.

Domain Consensus

In the formation process depicted in the Magnet Program, the Domain Consensus has two *physical* manifestations. The early one is the "Kick-Off" meeting, bringing all the potential participants to sit together and discuss the proposed activity, and agree on a domain of activity and scope of operations to be proposed for

---

[20] Triggering Entity has been explained on page 83, under the section "Formation".

the SRJV project. The second is the General Proposal submitted to the Magnet Authority, specifying the agreed-upon scope. Since the scope of operation is also determined by the activities and available technologies of the participating firms and academic partners, the scope presented in this document represents the agreed-upon group, as well as, scope of operation. Failing to submit that document would mean a failure to achieve Domain Consensus.

Formal Formation

From Domain Consensus expressed as the submittal of the General Proposal, the structured nature of the program takes over. This parameter is fixed, according to the regulations of the program. The resulting structure is also, to a very high degree, dependent on the structured nature of the program (as far as, the legal entity, its regulations and internal routines are approved and monitored by the authority). Therefore, it is assumed that once a SRJV project has reached Formal Formation, the performance and results are more dependent on the structure of the program and individual performance than on the earlier stages leading to this point. For the SP model, the relevant scope for analysis ends here.

DECISION PARAMETER

The processes described in both the models seem to show that the decision to join or not, is either following the approach by the Triggering Entity, or from the open call. In both cases, the decision has to be taken before the commencement of activities and therefore under some uncertainty; both regarding the scope,[21] and the identity of the other participants. The cases in which firms have been invited to join existing and ongoing projects are rare and have not been dealt with under any of the

---

[21]Scope of work for the consortium to be and the specific role of the firm making the decision.

proposed models. Therefore, the decision is made by the firm under uncertainty, where the risk is often high-core technology and strong competition.

The decision parameter is both very simple and very difficult. Expediency is the decision parameter translated into strategic benefit, both in the short and long/medium range. However, finding the balance for that decision parameter is extremely difficult and is ever changing. The entry into a CR promises great benefits strategically, but also has its dangers. The benefits are easily understandable, both economic and strategic, but so are the risks of such an action, which is therefore, especially in SRJV encouraged economically. The dangers are normally more complicated for the outsider, but very clear to the firms involved; the exposure of existing and future knowledge to external entities, and the exposure of certain inabilities to the same. In that aspect, it is important to know that here, once again, experience plays a major role— a significant portion of the projects approved in Framework Program 6 where continuation of projects in Framework Program 5 —which shows that for firms who have learnt to overcome the dangers, the benefits are great enough to try again. For better understanding of the decision factor, one has to consider the dangers and benefits of going in, as well as the dangers and benefits of staying out.

Box 6.1: Insiders and Left Out's

> In an electronics concentrated market segment, an RJV is formed to establish a joint technology platform, for the development of next generation electronics. Three of the four leading firms in the segment and most of the medium sized ones are participating. After two years, the RJV manages to lobby for the acceptance of their platform as the standard for that activity in the market. The non-participants cannot offer a competitive standard and cannot even form a counter lobby, as they are not organized in any form and do not have regular channels of communication. The firms within the RJV have the advantage of familiarity with the new standard as well as having a standard, fitting their development, manufacturing systems, and their quality control. The RJV participants managed to increase their competitive advantage; either to maintain their position or improve it, at the expense of the non-participants.

Inherent Dangers

There are several potential dangers to watch out for in a CR, especially when it takes the form of an SRJV:

1. Loosing government funding.
2. Being left out of a close club of market players; this danger depends on the market characteristics of course. The more concentrated the market, the greater the danger.
3. Being down-graded in market ties and being left out of a strategic partnership. As strategic partnerships are formed *against* someone, if you are not in, you are the one they are formed against.

Inherent Potential

The investment in the SRJV is very often rather heavy, and could be a real burden to the participants, especially, if they find that it is very difficult to get out. Often sanctions are heavier to members attempting to leave, than to outsiders. The knowledge resulting from the SRJV is subject to the Spillover Effect as any other research result. Therefore, in specific markets where the spillover rate is very fast, it is sometimes more economic to be outside the SRJV than inside. In fact, the determining factor is the balance between the spillover rate and the time it takes to get to the market, also expressed as the time it takes for the technology to translate into a product that can be sold in the market. If the spillover rate is faster, than the time to market, it may well be better to be left out than to pay the participation fee.

SUMMARY

Since the decision to establish Collaborative Research is of a strategic nature and is not only involving significant budgetary issues, but also dealing with core issues in technological sectors—knowledge and development—it has to be treated as part of a firm-specific strategy. The formation process of the CR is paramount to understanding the decision-making in the firm and the parameters influencing it. The formation process is described for two forms of CR by using two models.

In this chapter, the decision process and different strategic parameters have been identified and discussed. The importance of the sector and its parameters have been discussed (concentration, other consortia and so on). Once such a step has been taken, the firm needs to follow through or according to pre-established milestones, decide to withdraw. How to live inside a Collaborative Research Project will be discussed later on in the book.

7

The Decisive Role of Intellectual Property

Up to this point, the issue of Intellectual Property Rights (IPR) has been at the background of the discussion. Like the tiger in the jungle, it was there—one could feel or hear it and perhaps see a glimpse, but it was never in full view—and discussed and analyzed. In this chapter, I will analyze the importance of Intellectual Property (IP) as a strategic asset, but also as a commodity, and will relate to different aspects of it. I will relate to IP ownership, utilization rights, protection, and touch the issue of publication. I will also describe the need for understanding the different roles of the IP in different industries, and how the restrictions on IP protection can influence different industries. At the end I will give some examples of IP regulations from existing programs. The role of IP and relevant rights (IPR) cannot be exaggerated when dealing with collaborative research. IP being in essence, defined and packaged knowledge, is one of the most important (formal) reasons for the existence of CR. Therefore, its expression in IPR gains similar importance.

DEFINING IP

The definition of IP is most crucial for any project or program discussed here. The main purpose of a collaboration is the creation of such an IP, and in a form and format that can both technically and legally be utilized by the industrial partner (or other industrial parties), for measurable economic benefit. *What is*

Intellectual Property is the most crucial question, however, it is very difficult to answer. The difficulty in the answer lies in the practical repercussions resulting from such a definition.

> **Box 7.1: Academy–Industry IP Agreement**
>
> In a specific national program, the Industry is required to co-sponsor basic research projects, performed in the Academy. The Academy is required to transfer the resulting IP to the Industry, without further financial support; the industry in turn will be required to pay royalties for the use of the knowledge. The Industry and the Academy both agree that only, knowledge that is patentable will be considered IP under the program.

In the short theoretical example given in Box 7.1, we see that both Industry and the Academy agree to limitations on the definition and scope of IP due to practical reasons. The requirements of the program, present demands to both partners, which in turn may lead to negative economic benefits for both partners. The industry, while aware of the potential benefit from teaching and guidance from the academy sponsored by the government, does not wish to make the definition of IP too wide, so as not to incur royalty expenditure above the minimum necessary. The academy in turn, is less than anxious to incur extra teaching and guidance expenses, and additional time investment, above the minimum required. Both would rather focus their resources on the creation of the knowledge: the main purpose of the program. Therefore, the task of defining IP is universal, the definition of the IP is not. The definition of IP depends upon the practical implications of the program taking into account several different parameters:

1. The principal aim of the program: Creating basic capabilities; advancing specific industrial sectors; improving the collaboration; and supporting Technology Transfer.
2. The resulting practices of IP transfer: Who should do it; what they do and to whom; and assisted by whom.
3. The legal background of the area of activity of the program: The definition of patents, the rights of ownership (Prof. Privilege).

4. Cultural issues: Including the accumulated past experience of former projects.

The definition of IP will, therefore, differ from program to program, even when dealing with national programs resulting from the same ministry, and will require special attention, and constant adaptation and change, as the environment for the potential partners change. The only important general characteristics that can be described regarding the different IP definitions are as follows:

1. They have to do with knowledge sometimes, but not always differentiating between new knowledge created under the program and previous knowledge the partners bring with them.
2. They always include some referral to patents, not always limiting the IP to patents, but at a minimum, mentioning patents as an example of IP.

The definition of IP is very important, as the nature of IP combined with some of the other parameters mentioned above, determines the IP rights.

IP AS A STRATEGIC ASSET

The fact that IP is an asset is no longer disputable. IP is definable, it can be sold, hired (licensed), has maintenance costs (patent dues), and its value could be boosted (further patenting) or depreciated by time or by technology advancement, or market shifts. IP is a strategic asset, not just a simple asset—a claim that needs further looking into—to substantiate. IP is for long-term usage (for example, patent life) as it creates a strategic advantage (monopoly on use), and can be used as an entry barrier for competitors or an entry ticket, for the owner. It is used for the development of products/services and can be used as the basis for strategic alliances. The importance of IP as a strategic asset lies in its implication; it requires long-term investment and the attention of the highest levels of management. In a knowledge-based society, it becomes fundamental to the firms operating in the society and therefore a central point of management and attention, as it touches upon or affects different departments and actions in the firm. The formulation and management of IP is the central issue of the activity and of the following sections.

FORMULATING IPR

The Intellectual Property Rights (IPR) are the basis on which the partners base their ownership and right to use of the IP is created and brought into projects under the program discussed. The example given in Box 7.2 will give a hypothetical description of a program and its IPR, in order to demonstrate, some of the important issues related to IPR.

Box 7.2: IPR

> A national program aims to develop certain Low-Tech sectors of the local Industry and to introduce academic research in those sectors, while introducing academic assistance to the firms in the sectors. The program finances projects aimed at the improvement of the technical and managerial skills of the firms in the sectors, by co-financing teaching (up to 100 percent financing of that) and required research (up to 100 percent of academic costs and up to 60 percent of industrial costs). Now, the program intends the Industry to benefit from the fruits of the project. Therefore, the IPR decree the following:
>
> 1. The IP belongs to the inventors.
> 2. The industrial partner has the right to use the IP, royalty free.
> 3. In case the industrial partner relinquishes the use of the IP, the Academy may license the IP to another local firm, under a licensing agreement, and in this case demand royalty.

The reasoning behind the IPR as shown in Box 7.2 is simple:

1. The authority realizes that most of the results will not be patentable, but rather practices and improvements in

processes, therefore, the ownership can and had better be left with the academy, to encourage it to invest effort in the work—which will have small, if any, academic value. This will also allow consulting firms (surely on the side of management) to participate.
2. In order to encourage the Industry to cooperate with the Academy and to embrace the IP coming from the Academy, and even on a more basic level, acknowledge that the Academy may be beneficial to the firms, the IPR allows the involved firm, royalty free usage of the knowledge. Since the research was performed utilizing public funds, the authority can demand that from the Academy.
3. Since the involved firms may reject the IP, and as that IP was created by public funds, the authority wishes to encourage the Academy to find another industrial user in case the original one declines to use the IP. The easiest way to do it is to offer further incentive—the royalty payable to the Academy by the external industrial partner.

In a full IPR description of a program, the process of declining time frames for approval, and the ability to license the IP to another firm without asking the first firm's approval would be specified in detail. Elsewhere in this book, the sectoral (for example, ICT and Biotech) differences related to IP are discussed. However, at this point, it is important to remember the following: as the importance of the IP varies from sector to sector, different IPR should also be applied to fit sectoral needs and practices. If the program discussed is sector-oriented, the IPR can and should be detailed and very specific. If the program is multi-sectoral, the IPR should be more general and should contain in fact, end targets and general goals, so as to allow specific projects to adhere to them, rather than try and by-pass them in order to reach the same end point.

The topic of IPR during personnel exchange, like sabbaticals is an often neglected issue when dealing with IPR issues in Academy–Industry. When a researcher who has been trained and has acquired reputation in a certain field goes to spend a year at another institute, or even at an Industry, should the results of the work belong to the host or to the original institute? With an increase in the awareness of the commercial potential of IPR for the Academy, the issue of the visiting researchers' discoveries is becoming a hot issue, and not only when the host is industrial.

Hence, it can be proven that the issue of IPR is relevant and influential in all research cooperation models and not just in the Academy–Industry. In the section that deals with the IP, it is analyzed in more depth.

THE OUTLOOK OF THE DIFFERENT PARTNERS ON IP AND IPR

The basic difference between the Academy and the Industry regarding IP lies in the ability to utilize the IP for economic benefits. The difference between the Academy and Industry relating to the ability to utilize the IP for non-economic benefits lies at the bottom of the regulations regarding publications. The IPR discussed here will be comprised of the rights relating to the definition, protection, ownership, and utilization of the IP, as well as, the rights and mechanisms related to the publication of the IP.

How can we best narrow down the difference between the Industry and the Academy related to IP? The Academy and the Industry can both own the IP in most countries.[22] So, ownership is not a problem, and there have been, mechanisms for settling ownership disputes ever since patents where invented. The problem lies in utilization. The industries can utilize the IP for economic benefits directly. It can translate the IP either into products, or into processes that can lead to direct economic sales. The economic benefits are so direct that several programs, when requiring return of the support given for the development of the

---

[22]Even when the ownership by-law is not held by the academic institute but by the faculty member personally—the Prof. Privilege.

knowledge, link it directly to the gains coming from the sales of a specific product resulting from the supported projects financed by the specific program. This is not a minor problem. It is important to bear in mind that the main purpose of the generic R&D is to create a *usable knowledge* for the competitive advantage of the Industry involved. The Academy, however, is handicapped in that field. Not producing products and selling them, the Academy can only utilize an IP for economic gains only by licensing it to the Industry, or spinning affiliated companies off. The difference between the utilization capabilities may seem a small difference, but it is a very major one. The limitation in the accessibility of the Academy to the market and product production gives the Industry an edge whenever economic benefits are discussed. The Industry is able to sell the final products, it can develop them, it can characterize the products according to market needs, and it can comply with industrial standards—having acquired that ability as part of the entry into a specific market. The Academy is always, by definition in another sector and cannot, or can ill afford to pass the entry barriers of each Industry sector in order to utilize a specific projects' IP. So the basic characteristic that makes the Academy such an attractive partner for the Industry, the non-competition effect, is also the basis for problems when discussing right of use of the IP and the differences between the Industry and the Academy in that respect.

Box 7.3: IPR–Different Partners

In a national Generic Research program (an operating program), the IPR recognizes the difference between the two types of partners. All the industrial members share the IP utilization rights on a royalty-free basis. IP derived from the academic members' research, can be used by the industrial members, but carries a royalty obligation to the academic members. In turn, the industrial partners can transfer their IP to third parties without limitations (maintaining the access rights of other members), while the academic members have to get approval from the industrial members before approaching a third party. The program stipulates that withholding such third party licensing stipulated a license request from the limiting industrial partner, and therefore shall result in a license and in royalties.

However, the Academy is no longer unfamiliar with the economic benefits originating from licensing, spin-off companies and other commercial collaborations with the Industry. The recent moves (for example, the Barcelona Declaration) have brought the issues of IP and resulting benefits for the economy—the Industry and potentially the Academy—into the limelight (with business development as the new role of the universities). The Academy cannot ignore the potential income resulting from such activities, especially in view of shrinking government support, directing more and more funds into industrial cooperation. Naturally, in cases where the technology leads directly to a product (not generic), the optimal IPR includes a detailed licensing agreement that specifies the regulation towards protecting the IP and the utilization of the IP.

BENEFIT OF IP TO THE ACADEMY: A SHORT PHILOSOPHICAL EMPHASIS

How can the Academy benefit from the cooperation? The IPR has to allow the Academy to benefit more than just covering the costs of the research. It should also benefit, potentially without limit, if the innovation resulting from the research is big enough. The IPR needs to show sensitiveness to the fact that the cooperation discussed in a collaborative program is one between un-equal partners, and try and balance the activity accordingly. Most public universities[23] are non-profit organizations, funded by public (regional or national) funds, for the benefit of the public. They are tasked with education, creation, and preservation of Knowledge. The third column of activity, the Technology Transfer, is the source of the moral question raised here. If by public funds, a new technology is developed, who should benefit from it—and how?

Transferring the technology to an industrial firm without any royalties or economic benefits, would benefit the firm but would

---

[23]Private universities funded by private sources are considered here as firms or industrial entities.

have negative repercussions on the public institute. The firm would benefit from state subsidy and more than that, private research organizations would be thrown off the market, as they would not be able to compete with state-sponsored research and royalty free licenses. That would be both unfair and in the long run, economically harmful. It is, therefore, in the interest of society that the universities claim a fair and real royalty for the knowledge transferred to the Industry. But within the universities, who should benefit and how? Accepting that the university research is performed for the benefit of all, the *spoils* should be directed back into the research. There are several ongoing examples in different countries for the mix of support for the research in the same field as the technology licensed; general research and research infrastructure of the organization, and general costs. There is also a basic acceptance that the researchers should see some benefit that would encourage them to deal with such activities. The examples differ in the relative quantity of the ingredients, based on national, cultural or regionally acceptable practices. It should be noted that the inventor benefit is much more open to question than the contribution to the research. It is often claimed that the researchers are paid to research and invent, and should not get extra pay. Moreover, in some countries where the researchers are civil servants, such benefits may create discrepancies, when some civil servants get extra pay for their work, and others (just clerks) do not. As it often is, the university that has paid and assisted them to get to their level of expertise, supplied them with the infrastructure and the workers, so it seems strange that they should claim a bonus or even ownership. On the other hand, as innovation requires an element of invention, a spark, and more than that, the will to go beyond in a search for something new, in most cases, all agrees to some benefit. The allocation to general research is also understandable for an egalitarian point of view. Without the support for the general research areas, which attract less industrial attention, they would be neglected and forgotten. Social Sciences and Humanities suffer from that predicament, and while no less important, would not benefit from the Technology Transfer activity without the general allocation.

Box 7.4: IP-Revenues

In a university with extensive commercialization activity over several years, the engineering faculty has acquired so much revenue that the pre-graduate students would participate in international conferences funded by the faculty. At the same time, the humanities faculty found it difficult to sponsor the participation of senior members of the faculty in seminars abroad. That situation was creating two classes within the university senate, which led to a social crisis in the university. To solve the problem, the revenues from commercialization were *taxed* to the benefit of the general university funds and distributed more evenly among the faculties.

DO'S AND DON'TS IN IPR

The most important thing to keep in mind is that entry into a CR project is done, in order to, obtain the Knowledge. That should always be remembered when designing a CR program. This means:

1. The IPR should be clear and fixed. In order for a program to succeed, and as obtaining the Knowledge is the main issue, each should know beforehand what is going to happen to the Knowledge, who is managing it in each possible case, and the economic conditions involved.
2. The Industry should be assured that it could use the results of the research, and under what conditions. Without that assurance, the Industry is taking a huge strategic risk. The nightmare scenario being, the development of the next technological breakthrough, to be used by the competitors.
3. The IPR should recognize that the Academy and Industry are unequal partners in their ability to utilize the IP, for economic gains.
   In that case, what *should* the IPR include?

   (a) Provisions for the protection of the IP.
   (b) Clear rules and guidelines as for the utilization of the Knowledge.

(c) Compensation for the Academy related to its inability to economically utilize the Knowledge without the industrial partners.
(d) Provisions to reduce spillovers (see Spillovers).

WHERE ARE THE DANGER POINTS? THE DON'TS

Any ambiguity regarding the ability of the Industry to use the Knowledge (preferably in an exclusive fashion—at least limited to the CR projects partners), could lead to a failure to attract the Industry and lure it into participation in the project. The Industry repellant is both, unsure IPR, and the chance of spillovers. The Academy repellant is to have a complete ban on all publication, which contradicts the core of the academic work: publishing. A less strong repellant is to have no compensation for the economic utilization of the IPR done by the Industry. There is no real conflict between the academic thirst for publications, and the industries wish for confidentiality, as long as the knowledge can be protected and patented. If the Knowledge is not patentable, and the only viable protection is secrecy, than a compromise has to be reached, else the whole CR program may end. In sectors/cases, when a compromise is not possible, the clearly stated guidelines for the program will prevent disappointments, from unsuitable applicants. Luckily, that is rare, as there are several acceptable solutions, as will be shown in Boxes 7.5 and 7.6. In any case, the authority governing should make sure that the partners in each project financed, have faced the publishing issue and solved it clearly in an agreement/by-laws. That can be achieved in several ways; if the project is formed as a legal entity, requires that the publishing procedure is laid out in the by-laws of the entity clearly. If the project is organized via a signed agreement, then it demands that it contains a clear and operational section regarding publication, and makes the presentation of the signed agreement a basic condition for funding.

Box 7.5: IP-Publications

A firm and an Academy joined in a proposal for a TT supporting program. They agreed, that any self knowledge generated by each partner alone may be published at the discretion of the inventing party. However, joint invention can only be published by mutual consent. This way, the Industry feels it controls all the knowledge directly related to it. The Academy, at the same time, knows that any thesis that is its own individual work can be published, and that it has not relinquished the right to publish.

Box 7.6: IP-Publications 2

In a large R&D consortium functioning under an SRJV program, the partners agreed to a publication approval process. Within that process, any publication is submitted to all the partners for approval. However, approval can only be delayed for one of the following reasons:

1. The publication contains knowledge owned by another party and not the publishing party. The owning party objects to the publication of its knowledge. The publishing party has to remove the foreign knowledge.
2. The knowledge to be published can and should be protected prior to publishing. In this case, it helps of course, when the SRJV program supports financially the protection of IP.

Here again the Industry feels that its IP interests are protected and that important knowledge will be preserved for its use. The Academy knows that it can publish, and that students can be incorporated into the projects and later be allowed to publish their theses.

It is very important to stress that a CR program should avoid any ambiguity regarding IPR, both the Industry and the Academy should know the solutions offered and acknowledge that their fears are reduced. That the Industry will be able to use the knowledge, on one hand, and prevent the spillover to non-partners. The Academy should feel its basic needs are protected, and potentially there is some economic benefit in the work.

WHO SHOULD DECIDE?

The most difficult question regarding the IPR relates to the question: *who decides*? The basic decision lies naturally with the originator of the program, normally the authority. But, there are several items that are to be decided during the project life. The managerial decisions related to the managements of the projects under the program require the management team to fill in the gaps in the by-laws, and the decisions that were left open, in order to preserve flexibility. Normally, decisions regarding publications, patenting strategy, and the actual transfer of IP are left to the management team.

The management team and its composition, as well as, the by-laws are paramount to the decision that will be made during the project life. A management team or process leaning towards the Industry or the Academy will naturally lead to decisions that will favor the relevant party. The only barrier to the rule of the management team is a well-described and specified set of by-laws.

Box 7.7: IP-FP 6

> In the Framework Program (Framework Program 6), the guidelines by the commission are very basic; they aimed at end results, (ownership and publication, for example) but not the internal processes. That leads to very different internal routines employed by the different consortia and the different management team for solving the problem encountered during the project life. Since the by-laws state the final results, some of the processes are simple enough to define, but there is a great variety. Regarding the topic of publication for example, some consortia have placed strong limitations on the process of publication, but have freed theses publication completely from the approval-process; others have left publication of self-IP free to the discretion of the partner involved.

WHO SHOULD DEFINE IP?

How should IP be defined and protected, and by whom? Any protection of the IP requires the cooperation of the inventors. It is therefore, in many cases, that the protection is left to the inventors (Porath, 2006, 2007), with compensation for the involved costs, coming as part of the financing of the projects (for example, Magnet regulations—see www.magnet.org.il). There are options to form a committee to decide the IP matters and to execute the protection. However, even when such committees are created (like the Framework Programs 6 and 7 projects), the actual action is left to the inventors. Any action regarding the protection of the IP[24] requires access to the knowledge and the ability to define and describe it in detail. Only the inventors can do this. So while the decision can be by the by-laws, committees or management boards, the actual action is left to the inventors.

> **Box 7.8: IP-Joint Ownership**
>
> In a EU Framework Program 5 project dealing with nanotechnology (a FET Open Assessment project), the research has resulted in a potential patent application. The inventors are two researchers from a single partner organization. They get the approval of the management committee of the project, and utilize the budget of the specific partner for IP protection. Before the full project could be submitted, one of the researchers has moved to another institute and this new institute is a partner in the full FET Open project. The research results that the two researchers obtained at the Full FET Open projects are patentable, just as were the results of the Assessment FET Open project. They get permission, but this time the IP is co-owned by the two organizations that also use their budgets to cover the expenses. The researchers have personally participated in submitting the patent applications.

SUMMARY

This chapter dealt with one of the most important aspects of CR, the Intellectual Property Rights (IPR). The main point of the CR is the creation of usable Knowledge. In order for the knowledge developed to be usable and in optimal conditions, it has to be protected, and have clear rules regarding the access rights to it as well. The discussion in this chapter, presented the issue of IPR, its

---

[24]Likewise regarding the publication of the IP.

important points and the Academy–Industry conflicts and gaps, with examples. The basic issues, as well as, the divisions of roles and responsibilities have also been summarized in this chapter.

The chapter declared that the most important thing to keep in mind, is that entry into a CR project is done in order to obtain the knowledge. We have gone into listing the Do's and Don'ts of IPR, when designing a CR program and also assessed the roles of the different players, with regards to IPR.

8

The Academy–Industry Troubled Cooperation

Much has been said regarding the cultural differences between the Industry and the Academy. The purpose of this chapter is to allow the reader to better understand the conflict, as a cultural conflict, and hopefully allow the reader to find acceptable compromises. In this chapter, I will describe the conflicts between Academy and Industry as expressed in Collaborative Research (CR). I will describe two working environments; one with research institutes and the other with the Industry. I will describe the culture of a research organization and its special contribution to cooperation with the industry in research. The description will be done via conflicts, in order to get the attention of the readers and elucidate the insights better.

THE NATURAL CONFLICT

The Academy–Industry conflict is a conflict between two cultures. The clash of values and outlooks creates a tension in the relations of the two cultures.

The Academic Culture

The Academy has at its core two missions (Porath, 2007): *to preserve existing knowledge and disseminate it*, that is the reason for the teaching; and *to create new knowledge and enrich the human understanding of the world.* The important value in research is the achievement of first class research results, which is normally done, by carrying out first class research. The requirement regarding the quality of the research reflects on the quality of the organization, the personnel, and funding it can attract and in the case of universities, the demand from pre-graduate and graduate students to come and learn there. The quality of the research is a basic requirement that can often determine the nature and survival of the organization.

How can the quality of the research be judged?

Very simply by other researchers in the field and by their ascribing to its publication. Hence, emerges the origins of the importance of publishing. If your work is published many times in important and valued journals, it means that the research you do is important and that your work influences (is cited by) other researchers. So, publishing becomes the basis for promotion, and an index of the value of the academic work, and therefore in many cases, mandatory for Master and PhD theses. In time, publication became a value by itself, so far that the academic system deems non-publishing researchers as non-existing (Publish or Perish). More so, to make sure that your article is published, you have to be the first to do so. But, there are many groups researching close topics, as the *hot* research questions are few.

How do you get to be first?

One of the leading characteristics for fast publication is discussion, and openness, which in time, becomes another basic value. The presentation of your work, in progress or complete, according to circumstances is very common. That is also the basis for much collaboration. There is little fear of theft because why steal ideas when you can work and publish together without losing any credit points for that. As the academic world does not seek economic gain through research, research in Academy, is based upon the relative interest of certain questions. It is true that grants and funding are important, but they are just the tools for getting the research done; employ students, get materials and equipment needed for the research, and other similar expenses. Thus, the academic culture is about interest, the freedom to peruse that interest, the openness and exchange of ideas and results, and publishing of research results. That openness also allows the researchers to easily cooperate with partners from other countries and from different disciplines. The advent of nanotechnology and Science is a strong proof to that ability. One of the important characteristics to be recognized regarding academic research is the way academic research is evaluated and checked. Academic research results are published among other things, in order to allow colleagues to repeat experiments, check theories, and discuss the results of the research, confirming or rejecting them. The ability to repeat and thus approve the research results is often the only approval check the research ever undergoes.[25] The research results will, in most cases, not be checked or tested within the academic institute where the publishing researcher resides, and certainly not in an administrative regular way. The checking and evaluation is done by the colleagues after publication, but more importantly, it is the publication process through the peer review and editorial reviews, which perform the evaluation check of the research results and its quality. This process emphasizes the fact that the academic institute will never exercise control over scientific articles to be published, or the scientific work of its faculty members.

It is sometimes misleading, but academic administrative positions, such as the dean, head of school, head of department, and so on, are not signs of control—but rather of responsibility for resource allocation, and where relevant, control over tuition responsibilities. The heads of academic units will not review the papers sent for publication by their unit members, as part of their responsibility.

This process does not mean that there is no control over the research results, and that anything can be published, rather just the opposite. It takes into account the fact that peers are scarce within any academic institute, seeking to have researchers covering wide areas, and therefore, with a little overlap. That means

---

[25]As in the case of "cold fusion" that is sometimes all that is required.

that for the research institute to exercise control, it would have to reduce its research scope and have many competing researchers within. Such a step could result in downsizing the number of topics covered to maintain a reasonable size. However, due to the competition over applications for grants and to reach leadership positions that drive the academic institutes and their occupants, we find the academic institutes housing members with minimum over-lap in their areas of expertise. It means that the faculty members should not be covering the same topics and thus are not experts in the research fields of their colleagues within the institute. The real peers of the researchers are in other places, and they carry out very effective quality control, especially in experimental sciences, where the ability to repeat and verify results is crucial. The control is very effective, as each researcher knows that the results will be checked by jealous competitors and therefore, the researcher must be certain of the results before publication. These competitors will be harsher than the potential head of department who knows the researcher for a long time and may be more lenient. The peers would love to reduce the competition by proving frauds, and mistakes. After all, they want to be the leaders in the field as well. So there is control, and a very strong one, as it is worldwide, and very difficult to escape. But it is not the academic institute that exercises it, but rather the publication mechanism. This also means that the academic institute cannot control the research output, and does not have the infrastructure or routines to do so. This point is often missed by the Government and Industry (for example, demands for warranty and indemnification for mistaken results). The ease of the peer review as a managerial tool for judging excellence is evident in the promotion process utilized by the academic institutes. By counting the number of publications a researcher has in leading journals in the field, (and utilizing even more accurately the impact factor of these publications), the administration has a valuation tool to judge the quality and quantity of research performed by a certain individual and compare it to others, without being the expert in the researcher's specific field. The administration now can accept promotions or career decisions regarding the researchers without any understanding of their field of research. In fact, they do so based on external expert opinions.

As the number of researchers participating in collaborative researches with the Industry increases and with it the number of scientists agreeing not to publish specific projects results, the validity of publication as an evaluation tool is diminishing. If a large percentage of the work is not published, it means that publication as a tool of evaluation is loosing ground as a reliable source for judging the quality of research being undertaken by an individual or group. Also, if there is a significant increase in patenting, in place of publication in scientific journals, it will mean replacing the world of science with patenting lawyers as the evaluators of the quality of research.

It will also mean that young researchers seeking promotion will hesitate to join such CR, as it may, under the current system, hurt their promotion prospects, while mature researchers will not have such reservations. Consequently, the young and potentially innovative researchers would be prevented from working with the Industry. It is easy to demand that the Academy changes its regulations and takes into consideration the work that is not published, but that is difficult for the administration, as it does not have the tools to do that. Therefore, we have two arguments; the first being that the young researchers are prevented from the work, hurting research performed with the Industry under CR. The second is that the easy way for the Industry to demand that the Academy treats patents and size of budget as equivalent to publication is difficult for the Academy, as they cannot compare them to other researchers with publications. The publication impact factor does not allow for that.

Publication also serves as a tool for deciding grant allocations. It is an important part of the researcher's CV. Without decisions regarding grant allocation, employment, exchanges and hosting and many others would be damaged. To change the system of academic evaluation, there is a need for deep systemic change and not a restructuring of priorities. It would require developing new indices, intermediate indices for the time being, and some new evaluation processes.

Figure 8.1 presents in a drawing, the conflict between reducing costs on the one hand, and the need for additional investments for the academy to give up publication as an evaluation tool.

Figure 8.1: Independent Evaluation vs. Reduced Personnel

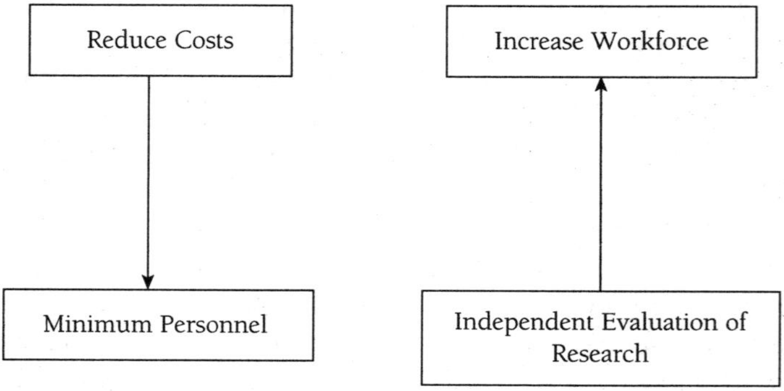

```
┌──────────────────┐         ┌──────────────────┐
│   Reduce Costs   │         │ Increase Workforce│
└────────┬─────────┘         └─────────▲────────┘
         │                             │
         ▼                             │
┌──────────────────┐         ┌──────────────────┐
│ Minimum Personnel│         │Independent Evaluation of│
│                  │         │     Research     │
└──────────────────┘         └──────────────────┘
```

Source: Author's own.

Another example of the cultural gap can be viewed in the different approaches to confidentiality. The work in a lab, in the Academy is very open, the research students and their professors form research groups, and while some may deal with different projects, they all share the same space, materials, and facilities. They tend to help each other in tasks that some are more proficient in than the others. That means that, while not everyone knows the details of the work of the others, there is a general knowledge in the lab regarding what each one is doing, or trying to do. Moreover, the internal regulation of the lab, like other aspects of academic work, is regulated solely by the head of the research group. The external administration does not deal with the internal management of the lab, and certainly cannot do so, on a regular basis. This means that keeping information confidential within the team is to ensure that this information would not leak out and be known outside the team or laboratory. They also do so, as part of their regular work to avoid competition from other teams. It requires special clarification and special attention by the head of the team to make it clear that some limitations should also be exercised within the team. Lab-internal compartmentalization is not obvious for academic teams. Even when safes exist within the lab, normally several team members would have access to them. Confidentiality in the academic world, within a research team is difficult, and any attempt at confidentiality can only be enforced by the head of the research team—this is the cultural manifestation of it in the academic world.

As a practical point regarding confidentiality, as the responsibility of the head of the research team, one should remember that in many CR's the funding authority does not deal with the researchers but rather with the academic institute or an affiliate. The demand for confidentiality would be an obligation (contractual or otherwise) of the academic institute or its affiliate, but that organ would be incapable of enforcing such a demand and would have to either oblige the head of the research team or else, just take the risk. In such cases as it cannot de-facto enforce confidentiality; the academic institute would try to avoid damages resulting from non-enforcement.

The two examples presented here aim to show the point of view of the Academy regarding two important points for the Industry when conducting research. The concluding section of this chapter talks about the resulting cultural conflict between the two, and it is important to remember that the contracting entity on the Academic side is not able to live up to its part due to the cultural structure of the academic world and work. Therefore, every solution or demand by the industry, while being legitimate by itself, cannot often be fulfilled in the real world. The changes required are structural and cannot be done easily.

Box 8.1: Academic Warranty

> In a national Generic Research consortium, where the relations between the partners are determined in the by-laws of an association formed, the industry demands that the academic partners assume liability for the research results presented by the academic researchers. The industrial logic

Contd. Box 8.1

Contd. Box 8.1

is simple: the Academy creates the results and it should stand behind it. Especially as the academic partners claim to have such a huge academic prestige and are so proud of their researchers. The academic partners (the contracting entities on behalf of the academic partners) explain that the researchers work cannot be controlled or checked by the administration, and therefore the administration cannot even assume liability in case some researcher decides, intentionally to do harm. This point of view is incomprehensible to the industrial partners, and a long argument ensues, resulting first in a break-up of the group and finally after arbitration by the funding agency, it is settled by compromise. The academic institutes take some risk, and the Industry comes out feeling that the Academy is trying to eat the cake and have it too.

Box 8.2: Academic Declaration

In another section with the same set of by-laws, the academic institutes declare (a demand by the Industry) that to the best of their knowledge there are no patents that block the usage of the results from their proposed research. That statement is for all members, industrial and academic. While it seems logical both to the funding authority and to the Industry, the Academy objects. The academic partners claim that patent searches are not normal in academic research, and that in most cases research is not considered an infringement of the patent rights. The academic researchers are not used to checking it and cannot be made to deviate from their usual way of doing research (or the entity cannot be liable in case they do not deviate). Once again this point seems very strange, and the Industry asks: Do you not control your researchers? Which is answered: No, we do not control how they do their research. Once again the solution is a compromise that takes into account that the academic research needs to be checked by the Industry before it is put into use.

The next section describes industrial research. As will be shown, it differs significantly from academic culture. These differences are the source for the conflict that appears whenever the Industry and Academy have to collaborate and there is an evident use or application to the results. This dependence on publication is also the source of resistance of the Academy to any limitations on publications, and not just obstinacy.

The Industrial Culture

The industrial culture is based on one principal: making money. Economic benefit can be derived in many ways, but research done in the industry is done for increasing the ability to extract that economic gain and translate it into money. In the industrial world, research is not a value by itself. It is a tool for creating the products and processes that create the main value, that is, economic gains (profit may be more precise, but in order to be generally accurate I will refer to economic gains). As a tool in a system that is based on economic values, research is often viewed from an economic point of view. In some sectors, it is viewed as an expense and in others, as an investment. This division is more than just semantics. Research as an investment means that it is considered as a strategic, long-term activity; general in the firms' actions and not linked to a specific product (in most cases). Correspondingly, research viewed as a cost/expense is a short-term (closer to or actual development), tactic and linked to a specific product or economic gain. However, in all industrial enterprises, research is viewed as a tool. Even while it serves as a product (for example, engineering firms), its main function is to supply the economic gains. The economic view of research, determines its characteristics for the industry. It is directional; it is aimed at solving a problem or offering a solution to it, or some advancement that will offer a strategic advantage. It is never entirely curiosity driven, free and without an end purpose or visible utility. Sometimes the utility is far away in the future (for example, HP and Nano science), but it is always there. The far away in time benefits are normally linked to technologies, long-term research, and therefore own a strategic character. The sectoral outlook and the mix between long-term and short-term research is a matter for discussion elsewhere. The industry will research in directions that are acceptable for the future of the market; will subject the research to the restraints of regulations and code of the sector, or the market; and will test the results not against their scientific value but against their economic potential. The most wonderful technology or discovery is just a cost, as long as it is not translated into a marketable product.

Box 8.3: Impressive Discoveries

> The Noble Prize is given to inventions that have had a lasting effect in their field. When looking at most of the most impressive discoveries, we see that they either academic in nature, or free research, or were accidental results. One would argue based on this knowledge that real changes in the environment and even in the market place can occur only by discontinuity points and break-throughs in the research performed. It would seem in fact that in order to discover the great next thing, the industry should perform academic research.

The open discussions of the academic world, allow for easier cooperation between disciplines, for the translation of ideas from one disciplinary domain into another, and for innovation. However, the partner most in need for innovation, the Industry, is the one operating in the opposite direction. The Industry tends to be secretive, wants absolute control and ownership of the knowledge, in order to get a strategic advantage over the competition in the market. But, the closer the Industry gets, the harder it is for it to be innovative or to become multi-disciplinary. One of the basic assumptions in this book is that while the Industry needs the academy, it does not know how to work with it.

THE CULTURAL DIFFERENCES SUMMARIZED

When the Industry has to comply with certain standards it requires special research methods to fit its needs. For example, when in the development of a drug, clinical trials are required with numerous participants for reliable statistics that amount of repetition is seen as special for industrial work. It is the same, in other fields, say, equipment development, in which reliability is an issue and the equipment need to be tested repeatedly over many hours to see, when and how it fails. When the Industry requires the Academy to relinquish publication, and views it as a cultural aspect and not as a managerial necessity, it does not understand that publication is at the basis of the academic system; not as a "nice to have feature" but rather, it is an administrative and managerial necessity. Otherwise, how would the academic administration decide regarding promotions when publications will no longer be equalization tools? Relinquishing the publication as the basis for scientific research evaluation will require a systematic change in the academic system as a whole.

The main cultural difference is that while the Industry may present a hierarchical structure all the way to the top, the Academy presents a hierarchical structure only up to the level of the head of a research group. From that point upwards, the hierarchy exists only for administrative purposes and not for scientific issues. Therefore, the sovereign unit in the Academy is the research group, but that is not a legal entity. This discrepancy in the structure is sometimes difficult for the Industry to comprehend. The Head of Department has no control over the research performed in his department, moreover, as this is a rotational role in most institutes, it means that for reasons of internal politics, the freedom of the heads of research groups is protected by the department heads and the levels above them, as the roles will be reversed in time. For confidentiality to be enforced, for control over the content of publications, for the delivery of the work contracted, the responsible party is the head of research group. While in most cases (for example, EU Framework Program projects), the contracted party is the research organization, the entity that has no real control over the actions of the research group. This shows lack of legal option. While similar demands in the consortium agreement show not only lack of legal options but also little understanding of the way the Academy works. On the Industry side, this approach makes perfect sense.

When dealing with CR, one should bear in mind that on top of the cultural differences between the Academy and the Industry, there exists also the conflict between two partners or any two different entities.

SUMMARY

In this chapter, the cultural differences and their implication in CR have been described. The structure and culture of the Academy were contrasted with those of the Industry to explain the resulting conflict. Most of the conflict areas can be easily resolved if the two types of partners better understand each other.

It is not only the Industry that fails to understand the culture and function of the Academy, but also the government or the relevant authority often makes that mistake as well. The Academy and Industry cannot be treated in the same way regarding responsibility and accountability, as the different structures and cultures often dictate a different authority and responsibility for similarly named organs in each. The difference was demonstrated regarding the role of Head of Department in Industry compared to that of the Academy.

9
Government: The Silent Partner

This chapter describes the role of the financing authority and the particular role of SRJV programs, but will also mention that government intervention is not always called for, and if required is at its minimum. The role of the government is definitely an important one; it is absolutely necessary, by definition, when dealing with the SRJV. The role of the government is that of an indispensable partner, even if at times, it seems to be negligible. The governing of the projects and the adherence to principals of *Fair Play* allow for the legitimacy of the projects. The basic principal should be that in economic activities, the Industry has a better understanding of the market needs than the government can have. It is therefore wiser to allow the industry to lead the way in TT issues in that case. The examples of government support in the Bottom-Up and the Top-Down cases is shown and discussed. Before that, the economic need for government intervention to increase social benefit is described, leading to the preference of the SRJV over other joint research forms. The role of international agreement is described, as well as, the limitation and opportunities they offer. This is not a legal analysis, but rather a more practical economic view of these agreements.

THE GOVERNMENT RATIONALE REGARDING SUPPORT TO COLLABORATIVE RESEARCH

The Economic Perspective

All the economic models from Katz (1986), through Kamien et al. (1992), and onwards have shown the social benefit of CR. The models mentioned above have evolved and become more and more complex—adding additional parameters—in order to try and come closer to real life (Kamien and Zang, 2000). However, the fact that there is a social benefit,[26] has not changed. It is therefore in the interest of a party to see the economy as a whole in promoting that activity. If you add to that fact, the trend to invest ever more in the knowledge-based sectors,[27] as a tool towards further development of industrial sectors with increased competitiveness in world markets, the SRJV emerges even more clearly as a governmental priority. When discussing in Chapter 3, the Triple Helix, the role of the government as positive supporter was assumed as the basis for the discussion. It is now necessary to further discuss that point.

In his article Porath (2004) compared two cases in which government support, while having a positive effect, was expressed completely differently. That case illustrates that the form of support that the funding agency lends to the program should have a strategic fit for the goals of the program (beyond the economic aspect) as well as for the resources available, the business culture, and the general environment. This chapter will focus on the two partners and some variations involved. The role of the government will be further described in this chapter.

Regarding the economic perspective, research (Kamien et al., 1992) has shown that the most socially beneficial form is the RJV. However, since the optimal form, from the point of view of the firm is the R&D consortium, it should be the governmental

---

[26]That is to say that due to the activity, the prices in the market come down while still allowing both the firms and customers to buy more with less.

[27]See the Lisbon Agenda (EU Com 50).

responsibility to make sure that the form taken by the Industry is the RJV/SRJV. Such a result can be obtained by the financial support for such actions.

Another important issue when dealing with the economic aspect of government support is the issue of collusion. It is economically accepted that the government has to protect the public from collusion by industrial firms. This would necessitate making the program for SRJV supported, supervised, and controlled to make sure the cooperation stays in the R&D arena, and is not moving into other activities; especially not towards the ones that are market oriented. There are several mechanisms employed today, from direct involvement in the management of the projects and closed scrutiny,[28] to control by reports and auditing.[29]

The Political Perspective

It is in the interest of the government to be seen as acting for public benefit. It is, therefore, important for the government to show that the funding going for research is being utilized for the general benefit of the public. It is public money that is being given to the research institutes; however, they do not seem to be acting for the general benefit in any obvious way except for education. Government justification for investment in research relates to two kinds of research: first, the research performed by the government (through agencies, national labs, or other pure research organizations), and second, the external research it supports (universities, private sectors, and so on). The external research supported is both by academic research and industrial research. In order not to go into the domain of ethics and the preservation of competition, these will not be discussed here, rather assumed to be taken care off (the government level of intervention in business issues has always been a dilemma). It is not easy for a government to support businesses formally and under public criticism and to do so,

---

[28] Such as the Israeli Magnet Program.
[29] For example, the EU Framework Program.

without a legitimate explanation, not required by private investors. The economic models presenting the social benefit, supply that explanation. Moreover, even when an explanation exists, the government still needs to show that it does not support businesses as some sort of a subsidy, or, one that interferes with market fair play in any way. Balancing that and maintaining at least some control over the businesses, so as to prevent misuse of public funds. It is the benefit derived from the research, that is, of interest in this debate. The industrial research has economic benefits, it allows the firms to develop products, sell them, and generate revenues that allow them to employ workers, pay taxes, and perform other economic benefits for the society. However, the academic research supported is more difficult to be so defended (Rosenberg, 1990). It has become a point of criticism that academic research can produce benefits only if transferred to the Industry, and that in this specific case, there is a market failure. That market failure has led to the efforts, all over the world to improve the TT rate. While government investment in basic research is criticized, and checked, and industrial research support is ethically controversial, at least regarding the firms, the investment in TT tools is welcome. When viewing the SRJV from that point of view, the basic benefit becomes obvious. The SRJV has a better chance for ending with a utilization of the knowledge, especially if the knowledge is developed as generic and complementary.

Figure 9.1: Basic vs. Applied Research

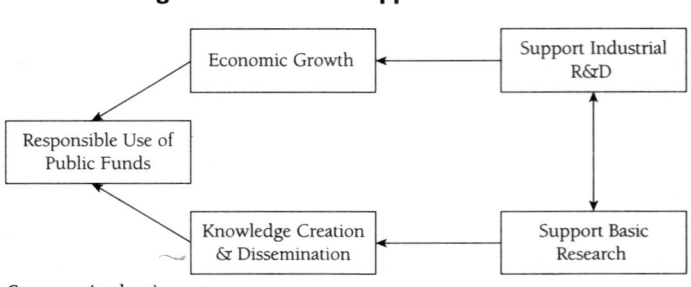

Source: Author's own.

Figure 9.1 has been studied in detail in the following text.

Public Support to Business

The government support to businesses has to be seen to give the entire economic sector and more directly society, some benefit. The funds that are used for the support of businesses could have alternatively been used towards other socially beneficial purposes such as education, health security, infrastructure, and so on. Whenever the competition over government funding increases and the cuts in governmental budgets increase, then the need to have the support of businesses based on un-contested explanations also increases. There are, additionally known benefits to the creation of Knowledge, the result of basic research (Rosenberg, 1990). After all businesses, not just in Laissez Faire countries (such as the US) are deemed to be entities well endowed with the ability to support themselves, and not among the entities requiring the protection and assistance of the state (or aspiring to that state). Economic research has shown that the social benefits of SRJV is positive and that it is the most positive of all the forms (Kamien et al., 1992) and, therefore, the industry should be encouraged to take it over other options. Additionally, the flourish of the High-Tech industries in the 1990's and the economic growth that came out of it, have made these industries worthy of support in the public eye. The governments today need not explain why they should support the industry and help it in R&D—that is, well understood, and can easily be explained (see Figure 9.2).

Impartiality of Government Support

One aspect that all governments have to reckon with, when dealing with support to private businesses or even to public ones, is the issue of impartiality. Impartiality is not to be understood as not giving any firm an advantage, but rather as having well-developed and accepted criteria for awarding the support. The issue of impartiality is important, especially, when regarded from a political point of view. A support program that does not have a clear set of criteria—undisputed and accepted—as the basis for attaining the desired social benefit, would not last. Not only would internal political resistance be focused on it, but it would

Figure 9.2: Authority Influence from Consortium to SRJV

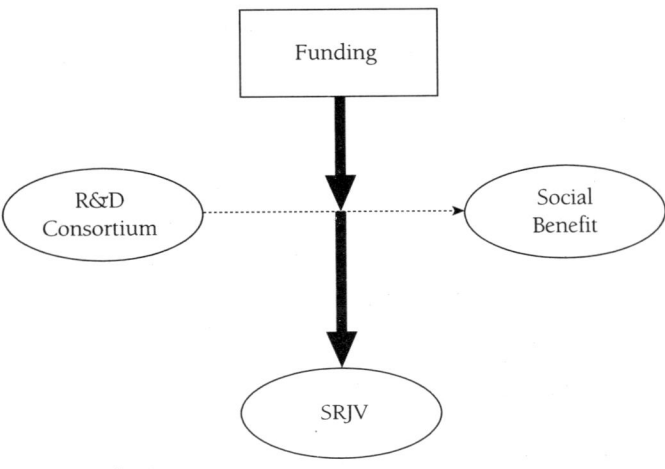

Source: Author's own.

also draw international criticism and perhaps even sanctions. The basis for the criteria would have to be that the firms awarded the funds (or partaking in SRJVs) would be those seeming to be able to best attain the desired goals. The criteria should also be seen to be utilized by a professional body that would be at least partially removed from the political aspect, and be seen to be professional. As will be seen in Box 9.1 and in the next section this is not so difficult to achieve and many governments have managed to do that.

Box 9.1: Eureka

> The EUREKA program is a good example. In order to avoid the debate regarding the legitimacy of support, selection of projects and rate of support given (conditions like grant/loan), these issues were relegated to the states involved and their regulations. This practical solution allows for international cooperation while retaining national compatibility within each state support programs. It does, however present, as a validated basic assumption that each country has at least one support scheme that can be applied.

Government Control over the Projects

As can be seen in the section, "The Economic Perspective", the government needs to exert some control over the funds it distributes and the way it is utilized (to avoid collusion). It is also required that the government provides some sort of accounts for its spending of public funding. The fears regarding bribes and the fears against collusion would require that the government keep tabs on the proceedings. Even if the government is not party to any mishandling or negative intentions by the Industry, it should also, on behalf of the public prevent the Industry from doing so. This is not the paternalism that comes to protect the firms but rather the public whose funds the governments has distributed and this is a part of governmental regulation of industrial sections. The government, however, should also leave enough freedom in the project management for the industry, in order to avoid the trap of a centrally controlled economy in which the government will take responsibility for directing the industry into the future development, when it is the least equipped to do so. It is the Industry that has to manage the R&D of the project. The government has to make sure that, once approved, the project will go according to forecasted lines to attain the agreed goals or fail (Luukkonen, 1998). It is up to the Industry in the RJV to offer alternatives to technological failures and not the government.

An additional important aspect that needs to be considered is the nature of the government support. In the EU, and its member states, as can be seen in many EU and national programs, the approach is mainly Top–Down, the topics and areas to be supported are pre-defined by the government, and then a call for proposals under these definitions is issued. In the US and Israel, for example, the approach is more Bottom–Up. The proposals come from the field, and have to assure the funding agency, that they are the best and should be given the funding according to the specific program aim. While this difference may be deemed to be minor, it has a huge effect. As the government is only approving of the best suited project according to the program's aims, and the final benefits are described and initiated by the participants, the success index is very simple: did it reach the desired goals (exceeded them) or failed to do so? These goals in many TT cases can be commercial. When everything is Top–Down, and the government is having a hard time presenting the economic ability to utilize the specific aims of the programs, the governments or funding agencies, are required to use assessment tools, that assesses the work invested and not the final results. In many cases, this is less than optimal, and creates the need to use indices that are not very credible.

Box 9.2: Possible SRJV–Government

> The government of a specific state decides to support TT activities in all sectors, as a boost to the economy. It leaves the field of application, and one of evaluation criteria—economic benefit—open. Therefore, for new project proposals under the scheme, the economic benefit is derived, which must be credible and based on the complementary firm abilities. The government uses this in the evaluation and can after five years try and assess the economic benefit derived by the participants specifically, and society in general.

Box 9.3: Possible SRJV–Government 2

> In another state, the government has decided that it would encourage TT in the fields of Bio-Tech and Nano-Tech. It invests a lot of money, and has created support measures based on the activity of the universities in the relevant fields. The universities and some firms become very active in the fields, but as they are very far from the market, they can not show any economic results that are not directly linked to the support they got. The complication of the indices involved has a negative influence on the general activity of the universities and on some of the firms involved who in order to receive the funding have adapted their activities to, the form encouraged by the government, but that is far from the market needs. The government is very frustrated, as it seems that while it is pouring a lot of money in, it has little positive effect.

The main government failure, in the example given in Box 9.2 is, that the markets for these specific fields are very young and, therefore, very dispersed. The government has to therefore allow even more freedom to the firms involved in the definition of their priorities, as there are no pre-defined dominating technologies yet. Furthermore, the government is trying to lead the market, intentionally or not, in the direction it is interested in, and is in fact, working against the market forces. It would be thus recommended, that the government releases the hold a little, and allow enough Bottom-Up approach dominated guidelines for action to appear and to allow the market to dictate the projects. That would allow one to concentrate on end results and not on effort, and will allow for better commercial results. The governmental control over the expenditure should not be hampered by this, as the government may impose the partial funding regulations and enforce the eligible costs concept.

THE GOVERNMENT DILEMMA

While this discussion may have given the impression of a criticism on the way some governments manage their SRJV, this is not the intention. Governments operate within sets of constraints, which dictate their actions. In this discussion, I mentioned the difference between the Israeli system and the EU Framework Program. The Israeli system can operate more easily Bottom–Up, as it deals with a relatively small country, with a limited number of firms, and a small number of research organizations. Moreover, it can afford to hold a team of semi-permanent evaluators to evaluate different proposals and go into the specific checking of each firm submitting a proposal. Therefore, it can allow a firm to suggest ideas for projects that the firms believe they can execute and later (directly or indirectly), bring to the market. The cost benefit ratio, including the cost of checking the suitability of the firms to fulfill their obligation is small enough. For the EU Commission, with such open proposal systems, it would be impossible to manage the Bottom–Up approach, without extreme administrative cost increase. The evaluation of proposals without predefined subjects would make evaluation very difficult; add to this, the need to check firms and research organizations in the member state,[30] which would increase the cost even more. Even if restricted just to the EU member states, the programs need to cover 27 member states with different languages, millions of Small Medium Enterprises (SME's) and hundreds of research organizations. The resulting complexity would make such a task costly, as well as, difficult to manage. It is therefore logical that the EU Commission has resorted to selecting topics, diminishing the pre-check process and other measures. The Commission uses associations and different other organizations to derive the *Hot Topics* for the future programs. This is a result of a set of constraints. There is however, one suggestion to make: in the ICT program since Framework Program 5, there has been a sub-program called FET (Future Emerging Technology) that allowed for long-term CR without visible use in the five–eight years open topics proposals to be submitted. There was an attempt in Framework Program 6 called Newly Emerging Science & Technology (NEST) to extend the FET into other programs, which failed, but I would recommend trying again, perhaps not for all other programs together, but specifically for each sub-program in the EU Framework Program Cooperation pillar.

THE WTO PERSPECTIVE

The governmental support for Industry is liable to criticism if unfair regarding competition. The government is required to demonstrate the need to leave the market place open to free

---

[30]Add to the 27 member states the associated countries and the third parties that for political reasons were added, and the picture becomes even more complex.

uncontrolled competition without giving an advantage to any firm. Firms are supposed to lead their strategies and competition without government support, direct or indirect. The support to sectors in R&D is considered to be part of the development and infrastructure investment of a government and not specific support. Moreover, like infrastructure, R&D support is not considered as interference in the market place competition. It is in fact one of the single areas where assistance can be given to a single firm, as well, to an entire sector, without impairing the competitiveness with others. However, some guidelines are recommended. The kind of financial support given is dependent upon the distance from the final product and the risk involved.

Basic Rules

Assistance given should be controlled and should be limited to assure maximum potential utilization and social benefit without hurting the free competition principle. So far, that would follow these basic rules:

1. Financial support is limited to part of the expanses, that is, controlled in two ways:

    (a) Only part of the expenses is recognized as eligible for financing.
    (b) The financing is limited by a top percent possible, and is given not as pre-financing, but as return on actual expenses.

2. Depending on the distance from the final product, the terms of the financial support can be given as a loan or as a grant. The grant is normally issued to wide scope research as close to basic research; when the results are shared among several partners, the loan given for development efforts to specific firms.

PROBLEMS OF GOVERNMENTAL FINANCING MECHANISMS

The financial mechanisms offered by governments are limited in scope; however, they include several special aspects for collaborative research. The example given in Box 9.4 will illustrate some of these problems.

Box 9.4: SRJV Finance-Magnet Program

> The Israeli Magnet program finance Generic Research of academia and industry intended for development of technology platform for and industrial sector (see Appendix to Chapter 3). The financial support model of the program is relatively simple. The Industry can get up to 66 percent support (as grant) from the government and the Academia up to 80 percent. The Industry is required to fill the gap to 100 percent for the Academy. The program imposes strict limitations on the eligible costs: salary cost up to a limit, equipment eligible only as specialized (as defined in the program) equipment, or otherwise only depreciation according to a predetermined rate is approved as expense and more. The Industry also needs to support the cost of the legal entity established for the project. The cost includes management costs, the information center and other project costs. These costs in addition to the support for the Academy can in some cases reduce the actual support for the Industry, to about 50 percent. More interesting than that is the way the firms actually receive the money. The project receives an advance that is divided between the partners after deductions to the Academy costs and the RJV costs. The firms therefore do not count as support the funds that they should get according to the letter of the program (66 percent) but the actual funding the receive.

We can see that some of the problems arise from the need to give support to two different kinds of sectors, Industry and Academy. There is a need to limit the support to the firms in order to make sure the program can withstand criticism and will not seem to interfere with the competition in the market place (see Table 9.1). The Barcelona Declaration in the EU has been investing a considerable effort to achieve the two goals mentioned; the 3 percent of GDP invested in R&D annually, and two-thirds of that from the private sector by 2010. Each country member in the EU is doing its best to attain that, and the EU is trying to promote EU wide measures (changing the structure of Universities to increase cooperation with the industry, the introduction of IC reporting in SMEs and more).

Table 9.1: Benefit and Dangers in Supporting SRJV

Benefits	Dangers
Improved competitiveness of the industry	Appear to maintain fair play towards all firms and sectors
Economic development	Alternative use of public funds
Improved utilization of research infrastructure	Long-term investment—politically risky compared to short-term actions
Increased social benefit	Social benefit difficult to identify

Source: Author's own.

SUMMARY

The role of the government is definitely an important one and is absolutely necessary, by definition when dealing with the SRJV. The role is that of an indispensable partner, even if at times, it seems to be negligible. The governing of the projects and the adherence to principals of *Fair Play* allow for the legitimacy of the projects. However, even in that case, the government approach can make the difference between success and failure. The basic principal should be that, in economic activities the Industry has a better understanding of the market needs, than the government can have. It is therefore wiser to allow the industry to lead the way in TT issues in that case. The examples of government support in the Bottom-Up and the Top-Down cases has been shown and discussed. Before that, the economic need for the government intervention so as to increase the social benefit is described, leading to the preference to the SRJV over other joint research forms. The role of international agreement is described, as well as the limitation and opportunities they offer. This is not a legal analysis, but rather a more practical economic view of these agreements. The problem of the government financing mechanisms is also described.

10

How to Run a Successful Collaborative Project

This will be the first among others, hands-on advising chapter in the book. It will be written from the viewpoint of a project manager who has to ensure that the participants and the financing authority are happy, so as to assure his position and future. The manager needs to keep rigid financial management in an ever-changing research environment characterized by high risk, constant change, and uncertainty. I will describe the steps and items to look out for, without referring to any specific program, but will make a program-needs list, as the items are spelled out. After all, the thing to realize is that CR is good and beneficiary for its partners. All that is required is proper management. As there are many project management and research management texts available, this chapter too is going to provide a general overview but will not deal with the technical-scientific management of the CR project. It will deal instead with the mechanism and routines to be considered administratively, when dealing with a CR project.

BASIC REQUIREMENTS

The basic requirements should be divided into the following categories:

1. Central management

   (a) Technical
   (b) Administrative
   (c) Financial

2. Partner management

   (a) Technical
   (b) Administrative
   (c) Financial

3. Interfacing

   (a) Internally
   (b) Externally

Central Management

Technical

An experienced technical manager, specialized in the technical field of the CR should be appointed. However, a technical person will require even more administrative support than a non-technical person, as his major focus and management skills would be best used by promoting the technical progress of the project.

Box 10.1: Overcoming Financial Management Problems

A firm, in a national Technology Transfer project, needs some technology to complete a line of products. That technology exists in the Academy and the firm thinks it has identified the correct technology. It then wants to validate the technology and license it, in order to develop its new line of products. To do that, the firm appoints one of its engineers to head the project. The main point is the validation. Since the engineer is good, he is perfect for the technical work, and this part proceeds well. However, the administration in the firm cannot understand the type of project. Is it a purchase of a sub-contractor's work? Is it an internal (budgeted)

Contd. Box 10.1

Contd. Box 10.1

> development project? The firm recognizes the problem early on and deputes a finance assistant, from the firm to the project. The engineer and the accountant cooperate well and the project finishes well on time. The firm decides to continue working with the program in the future.

Administrative

An administrative manager would have to be appointed, to assist the technical manager and to liaison with the financial activities and the different assisting/supporting services.

Several assisting/supporting services would be required:

1. Basic legal advice.
2. IPR strategic advice and support services.
3. Personnel and general administration assistance.

As the IPR management will be part of the administrative management, the appointed administrative manager will have to take care of it.

Financial

The management of a CR requires a good administrative backing. As in most cases, the CR will be supported by an external agency, which will require financial reporting, and probably more than once. The specific financial regulations of the funding authority are less important, than realizing, the cooperation from the partners in managing the project financial needs.

Partner Management

Technical

The topic of Partner Management in a SRJV is complex. In all SRJVs, there are internal routines for cooperation among the partners and for management of the work. If the SRJV program requires the formation of a legal entity, these routines will be included in the by-laws and regulations of the entity otherwise, they will be included either within the regulation of the program or in a direct agreement between the partners (compatible with the regulations). Whatever the situation, the manager should make sure that the regulations and the internal routines required for the smooth operation of the SRJV are in place and known to the partners. The regulations should include the responsibilities among the partners (to each other), and towards the external world (the funding authority and anyone else deemed relevant). The agreement, by-laws or similar, should include the technical issues regarding the technical management of the project, deliverables, decision making, and reporting processes. Only by having these routines understood and accepted by all, will the project manager be able to direct the SRJV towards technical success.

Administrative

Following the previous section, the administrative issues and regulations should also be made clear. This can be more complex. In SRJV projects, the main interface between partners from the proposal preparation phase and onwards is done among the technical people. It is the technical staff who does the writing and preparation, and later the research work, including the preparation of the deliverables. They normally interact on a regular basis and create both, working routines and relational assets, very fast. The administration in each partner organization is normally at least one degree removed from the project. They seldom, if ever, meet, and would normally (especially first time in the SRJV program) treat the SRJV work as if it was one of the projects they are used to. In many cases, over-work and a lack of understanding of the differences between the SRJV and other activities in the organization, tend to reduce the understanding the administration has in managing the SRJV. It is therefore, for the project manager to ensure, not just contractually, but also by training and explaining, that the administration understands the specific regulations of the SRJV; setting it apart, and if required, create special routines within the specific partner organization that will allow compatibility, with the SRJV internal routines and the regulations of the SRJV program. Failure to do that could result in major problems for the smooth management of the SRJV, endangering the completion of work, and at best, demanding a major share of the management effort of the SRJV.

Box 10.2: SRJV Finance–Complications

> In an SRJV project, the administration of the firm leading the SRJV failed to understand the differences between the SRJV and purchasing knowledge from external sources. It failed to make the changes required in the internal processes. One of the other partners was an Small Medium Enterprise (SME) and could not get funding from the SRJV financing authority (due to regulations regarding the value of the firm and the size of the budget) for all the work it was required to perform. The leading firm agreed to use the SME as sub-contractor and share the cost with the other partners. The work demanded that the leading firm purchase from the SME some work and pay for it and later get funding back from the financing authority. The administration decided to treat the issue like any sub-contracting activity. In order to pay the SME, the leading firm required either an order for purchase of the final product (as if purchasing a component from a supplier), or a research contract, directly between the two. It would not accept the by-laws of the SRJV, the work-program or any other similar documents. As they would not pay, the leading firm could not show the expanse and claim reimbursement from the financing authority, and the SME after a while, could not go on working without getting paid. The work was in danger of stopping. Since, even after a long series of meetings and training, the leading firm did not change its internal routines, the financing authority had to intervene, in order to get each payment through. This caused internal tension and got in the way of the work.

Financial

The financial regulations regarding work in a SRJV, similar to that of administrative work, require training and adaptation. For firms not used to getting reimbursements for R&D expenses (including, or not, consortia management costs), the adaptation could be complicated. Reporting is more often a major problem. The marriage between the R&D (or, the technical one) and the financial or accounting department, is a problematic marriage for all types of organizations, profit oriented or not. However, it is important for the successful completion of the project. The funding authority cannot normally approve of payments without evidence of progress (it is, after all, accountable for responsible spending of the funds), which includes reports and other control mechanisms (for example, visits and tours, information days and displays, as well as, audits). There is often a demand to link the reported expenses to the progress. While the R&D department may be used to reporting total expenses, here, they need to differentiate the specific costs of the project, and have to adapt to the SRJV way of reporting the expenses, which may be different than the usual reporting the partner uses and may require special preparation for the two. The project manager should also ensure that the partners (those without prior experience with the SRJV program) correctly instruct their finance personnel and would be advised to check specifically with them. Anticipation and prevention would be recommended for the project manager. Waiting for the reports to see that there are problems would result in payment delays and dissatisfaction on the side of the partners.

Box 10.3: SRJV Finance–Complications 2

> In EU Framework Program 5 project, one of the partners cannot get used to the EU demands for reporting. The partner is a large research organization, but it has little experience in the EU Framework Program, and tries to implement the reporting protocols it normally has. That change in the reporting style creates extra work for the coordinator, and worse, results in some reported expenses not being approved. The commission instructs the coordinator to reduce the payments to the partner, and clarifications are required. After three long years of dialogue, some of the expenses are not approved finally. The partner's internal culture deems the EU Framework Program projects, complicated administratively, making it less attractive than other options. The coordinator shall no more wish to include that partner in future projects, and feels that its reputation has suffered.

Interfacing

While it may seem trivial, many SRJV project managers spend time and effort (for example, sweat) regarding interfacing. One should bear in mind that the management of an SRJV is like a management of a web of partners—some of who have never worked together before, have suspicion and trust barriers to cross, and relational assets to develop. There are two kinds of interfacing, one with the SRJV partners (internal), and one with the rest of the world, including the funding authority (external). The differences and the importance of each are explained in the further sections.

Internally

The internal function of the SRJV depends on the interfacing among the partners. Since in the SRJV each partner performs his part alone, the mutual work has to be done by transferring research results among the partners, as in an assembly line. If the transfer is not smooth or full, the project may well fail. It is the responsibility of the manager to see that the members develop relational assets and trust, up to a level, that will allow them to cooperate in a way beneficial to the SRJV. The manager should be complementing the rules of the SRJV program by giving clear rules regarding the transfer of research results, and prior knowledge, thus creating a complete set of internal routines for the SRJV program, hence, establishing internal routines for the SRJV.

Box 10.4: SRJV–Scientific Management

> In an EU project, one partner (T) had to produce a molecule. One part of each sample would be sent to partner (H) for special treatment, and the second had to be sent to another partner (E) for characterization. H would also send the treated molecules to E for characterization. T would also characterize the molecules crudely at his own facilities. During the first year, there were problems, the results T would get would be different from these E got, and H could not get a stable process for the treatment. These problems were solved by active interface (personnel exchange) among the three partners. A routine was developed for the documentation of each sample when it was sent to another partner to allow for the creation of a base line.

Externally

The interface with the external world is a complicated task for the SRJV manager. Sometimes, there is a need to publish the fact that the SRJV exists, and what it does (general terms). This can also be a demand of the program, resulting from the funding authority, who need to show where the public funds are going (for example, the Commission publishes the abstract and participants lists for the EU Framework Program projects it funds). These types of external world publications (for example, a SRJV website, newsletter, and so on) should be the result of contributions by all interested partners, but managed and controlled by the project manager. Here again, developing a routine for contribution, editing, and scrutiny is recommended.

Another type of external interfacing is the interface with the financing authority. The project manager should bear in mind that once approved and operating, the main interest of the financing authority is to have the project appear as a success. The appearance depends upon the goals and purposes of the SRJV program, and the specific goals of the SRJV. The authority would prefer to approve budget changes, timetables, and deliverables (as long as they stay within the SRJV program limitations and the goals of the SRJV), rather than have to close down the SRJV, and stop the financing. In such cases, the financing authority will carry at least, part of the blame. However, the project manager should understand that in order to be on his side and support him, the financing authority would have to be on board regarding the progress of the SRJV, and know what is going on. This can, and should be done, both officially (for example, periodical reports and the SRJV program demands) and un-officially (for example, emails and phone updates from time to time). This will allow the financing authority to know the problems early enough and suggest a course of action. The manager should try to overcome problems and get the authority's help.

Box 10.5: SRJV–Administrative Management

> In the EU project mentioned above, the project manager took care to update the project officer with the progress news, and consulted him regarding potential problems. As happens in many cases, towards the end of the first year review, it appeared that one of the deliverables would not be ready for that year, and would perhaps, be removed from the work program,

Contd. Box 10.5

Contd. Box 10.5

> as the research was developing towards a different solution. The project manager unofficially consulted with the project officer who advised him on how to prepare a request for change in the deliverable list, offering new deliverables resulting from the new course instead, and an amended research plan (there were no changes in the budget) before the end of year one. The project manager sent this to be approved, according to the procedures. At the time of the review, a few months later, the project was evaluated according to the new approved work plan and deliverable list, and got full marks for performance. Therefore, had the project manager waited for the review to show results, explain the required change and the removal of the deliverables, the reviewers and the project officer may have been able to help, but that would be more difficult and the project would have bear the stain of poor performance.

One should beware of the danger of over-burdening the authority. The authority representatives normally have to take care of more than one project at a time, and would not appreciate unnecessary information. The information should be real and contain the basics, to allow the authority representatives to ask questions or give advice. The official periodical reports can be more detailed.

WHO SHOULD MANAGE?

The CR has tangible goals. These are the program goals and the specific project goals. It stands to logic that the partner responsible for attaining the goals, the potential application, should be the leader. If the CR is market driven and the Industry is responsible for having marketable results, it is up to the Industry to manage the project. It is up to the application responsible partner to make sure that the end results are relevant to application, and are in a format and quality fitting the application.

Academic management of projects may end in the Industry, if they are not able to fulfill their basic obligations, and in time, it would kill the program. It is possible for the Academy to lead, if the research supported is very basic and advanced. This way the Academy is allowed to bring forward its flexibility and multi-discipline research abilities, focus on the long-term problems, and allow the partners to concentrate on application findings. The downside of this arrangement is that since the number of academic research organization is normally limited, and due to, their intensive involvement in research, they tend to have a lot of acquired experience with the different programs in their area, they end up with the managerial experience relevant to the CR programs. One of the reasons for the market failure of the collaboration between the Academy and the Industry is that the partner with the experience and expertise in management is not the partner who should strategically manage (and normally does manage) the Industry. This may seem like a paradox, but, in fact, it means that the formulation of a CR program requires the creation of a structured program that would be clear enough for the Industry, and have a framework that will allow for inexperienced project management to survive and achieve the intended results.

Box 10.6: SRJV-Management Demands

> The EU Framework Program is a classical example. As the Commission understood the need for expert project management, it created double safety guards. On the one hand, the project proposal must have a description of the project management—including a drawing of the management structure (all that is supported as part of the budget), which is part of the evaluation criteria—on the other hand, it should also have the double set of contractual agreements, the grant agreement between the Commission, and the consortium and the consortium agreement (the agreement among the members). Both agreements set the management and by-laws of the project before hand.

The authorities responsible for the programs often see the Industry as their main client and therefore often forget the other aspect, wherein the research organization are the most ardent participants in the CR programs. In fact, they could serve as the promoters, leaders, and educators for the CR program on behalf of the authority and help promote it.

There are two traps that need to be avoided. One is governmental management and the second is research organization management. The governmental management is obviously a mistake. It is widely known that governments do not do business well and therefore for them to manage CR, which is to have a business end, is evidently wrong. Moreover, it cannot be expected that one agency manages efficiently and with efficacy, the R&D over all technological sectors. In general, the results of the CR in R&D activities are to be used, they should be defined, or the requirements from them should be defined by the party, which is, supposed to use them. This party, that is, the utilizing party, should not only define the technical requirements, but also, the legal and IP protection. The research partner would have difficulties managing the projects according to specifications and requirements of the utilizing party. The research party would have to adapt to the business requirements and additionally, be culturally (see Chapter 8) handicapped, for managing a project with a business end.

HOW TO MANAGE?

This section deals with the management aspect from two levels: the authority level and the project level. From the authority level, it is important to assure enough freedom to the research performers, in order to, allow them to overcome obstacles and changes, both in the research and in the end market for the research results; and at the same time, maintain the research framework that helped the selection of the project for financing. From the authority point of view, what is important is the attainment of the project and consequently, the attainment of the program goals. The specific route, as long as, it is within the legal framework of the authority, should be less important. Therefore, the authority control or management should be *loosely coupled,* allowing enough freedom for the partners to operate, but allowing the authority the advanced knowledge to stop problematic steps, and maintain over all transparency and accountability. At the project level, it is important for the participants to be able to attain the goals of the project and the program. The success of the project is important on two aspects: utilization of the projects results for the strategic needs of the partner and for the track record. Thus, for future projects, the smooth management of the project is important.

This book does not deal with project management. However, some unique aspects should be discussed regarding CR project management. The involvement of two culturally different partners, under the supervision of the funding authority, adds special dimensions to the regular R&D project management. The funding authority adds one obvious dimension, the added burden of reporting. Since public funds are being used, reporting is involved and required. In two sided projects, there would be project internal reporting, including whatever reporting is required internally by the partners' regulations. In the CR, additional reporting is required by the funding authority. Since the funding is dependent upon progression according to the approved work plan, in most cases, there are two types of reporting involved; financial and technical reporting. That, by itself, may not seem a severe complication, but as it requires, that, two separate departments cooperate in reporting, it may require some internal changes regarding the organizational routines of the partners. Moreover, as the punishment for mistakes in the reporting could impact not just the reporting organization but also the other partner, it adds to the responsibility of each partner. This added reporting to the funding authority is therefore an additional burden to project management in the CR. It is often also seen as a sort of a tax. As the reporting does not seem to help promote the project, it just adds to the work.

Since the funding authority is involved, it adds one more dimension to the complexity of the project management. The project management will include not just project management, but also funding authority liaison management. The funding authority management is required to assure full budget support for the project in the short run, and the accessibility to future projects, in the long run. Well-managed projects are perceived, as such, and it is important that the positive opinion of the funding authority is created and maintained. The relations with the funding authority should be kept on a regular basis, and be free from the "I have a problem syndrome". It is better to report regularly, even off the record (finding the correct balance, so as not to burden the funding authority officials), and not approach just when problems or requests arise.

In most CR projects, the Industry leads, as it is responsible for the management of the results and for the application of the results through further research, up to the final product, or process. In that case, the Industry should solidify the end goals, but leave for the other industrial partners, as well as, the Academy, freedom regarding the work and the means to reach the final goals. It is a question of balance and of navigation, and not a clear and straight road.

There are several aspects of management to describe—the disciplinary aspects, the internal-external aspects, and the individual–group aspects.

The disciplinary aspects to the management deal with the issues of:

1. Scientific management
2. Financial management
3. IP management

The internal-external aspects deal with:

1. Internal management of the project, who does what and how, solving discrepancies between partners and resource allocation.
2. External management of the project facing the commission and the rest of the world; the financial and scientific reporting, adhering to the commission regulations and directives, as well as, liaison to the project members.

The individual-group aspects:

1. Managing the project, while giving freedom to each partner to manage his own activity.
2. Remembering that the group has a narrow domain for cooperation, while on another level, the partners may compete in the market, or be elsewhere occupied.
3. Remember that the project is short-term cooperation with potentially long-term lasting results.

SUMMARY

This chapter dealt with the management issues of the SRJV project under a SRJV program. The issues and problems presented, aimed to present the complex world of a CR project management and give some very general guidelines. Most of this chapter discusses the issues from the point of view of the SRJV project manager (for example, technical, administrative, and interfacing), while the *Who should Manage* and *How to Manage* sections, were discussed from a more general perspective.

11
How to Avoid the Pitfalls of the Collaborative Project

This chapter will describe the dangers of participating in a project from the viewpoint of the industrial partner and the academic partner. I will describe the actions to take to avoid these dangers, as well as, the signs to look out for when involved in such a project. Before defining the pit falls and later showing potential ways to deal with them, a definition of the point of view is important. In a classical Collaborative Research project, there are two types of partners involved, that are mandatory, and one partner, which is elective. The two inherent types are, of course, the Industry and the Academy, and the elective one is the governing Authority.

The government point of view regarding the pitfalls is very simple; avoid wasting money. The ways to do that can be varied and often depend on very specific national or regional situations and experience—this discussion merits a book by itself. The important point for the government to remember is not to appear to be wasting money. That is normally dealt with, in the program regulations by making sure that there is financial and legal accountability, and adequate controls. The second problem for the government, that is, the *impartiality factor* was mentioned earlier and it deals with competitiveness and its maintenance. Again, this is dealt with, within the regulations, normally in the approval process of the SRJV projects, but also in the regulations regarding joining and leaving the SRJV projects.

The most problematic points of view are those related to the inherent partners. Without solving apparent problems, the collaboration will not flourish and any program or private initiative will fail, due to lack of use. This chapter will deal with these two points of view and will end with the conclusion and recommendations for the interested parties in formulating a collaborative research consortia.

THE ACADEMIC POINT OF VIEW

When dealing with the Academy in CR, one has to bear in mind, that from the Academy point of view, a successful CR project ends with, as many as possible, strong impact articles. The more important the articles are, the better it is. By achieving that, the Academy advances its own purposes. The Academy in CR is looking for research, potentially for some connections and contracts for the future, but not for gaining strategic advantage. The danger the Academy would see, in such a case, is that cooperation with the Industry pushes it into doing development work or second-rate research, or the kind that has little academic value and little chance for high-rate publication that would bring academic prestige. In the Academy, most researchers would worry about that, as it would also hurt their chances in getting students and research grants for the research infrastructure of their labs. Thus, second-rate research for first-rate development is one point of worry. The second, stemming from the same basic fear, is the censorship of publication. When all that is over, there are other small things that are problematic. They become more problematic as the Industry tries to make the Academy simulate in its research for industrial development. These are the cultural differences.

Box 11.1: SRJV–Management Difficulties

In a SRJV, the Academy is obliged to work very closely with the Industry. The Industry appoints *liaison persons* for each academic research. One such person is very young and inexperienced in the ways of academic research and tries to direct the project he is liaising with, to do less basic work, and to provide sufficient repetition of an experiment for statistics required by the standards in the sector. The academic team objects to this. They agree to do some of the work, but not the repetition and the standardization required. After the liaison person applies enough pressure, the academic team retires from the project, and leaves the consortium. The team elects another topic for their research and finds financing for the work from another source.

The industrial liaison person is amazed at the reaction. He actually does not understand, why a request, that is, completely logical and understandable for an R&D department in any firm in his sector is objected to.

The will to maintain academic freedom and independence can be seen as the basis for the cultural differences. Moreover, the academia would not normally wish to control the research and its results, while the industry in most cases would.

Another potential problem is the ownership of the resulting knowledge. In a SRJV, the Industry contributes some of the funding and so wants to own the resulting knowledge. The Academy would want to own the knowledge from the following reasons:

1. The Academy developed it and, therefore, the knowledge belongs to it.
2. The Academy has a mission to improve knowledge creation for social welfare. It would like to own the knowledge to make sure it is used for public benefit (for example, avoid shelving).
3. Keep the options for future research and future publications unrestricted.

This point is special in that it tends to appear in Academic institutes that have Technology Transfer and CR awareness. This awareness is normally connected with high-level cooperation with the Industry.

THE INDUSTRIAL POINT OF VIEW

The Industry is interested in the collaboration for a very specific purpose. As a profit oriented institution, it needs to see that the results of the specific collaborative research project can be translated into economic benefits that outweigh the economic benefits it could generate based on the resources it has invested in the collaborative research project. By including the long-term and short-term economic benefits, we can also take care of strategic consideration in a very general way. Factors that are a cause of concern for the Industry:

1. Strategic aspects: Market share and competitive advantage.
2. Direct economic aspects: Increased sales and product development.
3. Licensing aspects.
4. Long-term capabilities: Entry into new and emerging markets.

Strategic Aspects

In an ever-changing technological world, the firms are in a constant race, to try and maintain or reach some sort of a competitive advantage that they will be able to sustain. That competitive advantage will allow them to maintain or acquire market share, increase or maintain sales that will eventually translate into profits. For the firms in the technological world, the clearest and most straightforward path to competitive advantage is through technological advancement. Technological advancement can be reached through research, and the easiest is to do something that the others cannot, or are not allowed to utilize. The more basic, advanced and innovative your research is, the higher are your chances at being able to turn it into a competitive advantage. That is the basic incentive for the Industry to cooperate with the Academy in research. The fundamental need of the Industry is to see that the end products are translatable by the industrial partner into the economic benefits it requires. The best academic innovation, if cannot be translated into economic benefits by the specific industrial partner, will not be used for the public good. The industrial partner will of course, select topics that are of interest and will either by itself or with authority assistance, make sure it has the potential to translate the end products into economic benefits. However, it will want to ensure that:

1. The knowledge is protected in the way it would like, in order to, maximize its potential competitive advantage.
2. That it owns or has control over the resulting technology, and to a certain aspect, the future developments of that technology.
3. It owns the technology and understands it deeply enough to utilize it.

The pitfalls appear in the contact points with the Academy where the three basic aspects above are conflicting with the Academy needs. The protection of the knowledge would conflict with the Academy demands where the protection method involves secrecy. The academic world (see "The Academic Point of View"), requires publication and as such would want to publish the research results. This point could create tension and that would lead to conflicts between the partners. The cost of the protection is not so problematic, as patenting for example, is the preferred method of protection. The patenting strategy is easily agreed upon, and as here, both partners normally would have the same interests and would gladly assist each other.

Ownership is also a problem as the Academy would normally like to retain ownership of, at least, its share of the invention (see "The Academic Point of View"). This can however be solved by the Academy giving the industrial partner an exclusive license for their part. This will allow the industrial partner to have de-facto complete control over the technology,[31] still keeping open the possibility of the Academy to re-license the technology in case of dissolution of the industrial partner.

The active ownership of the technology and the ability to actually utilize it, is paramount for the entire project. The industrial partner will need to make sure that during the project, the transfer of the technology occurs. That is not complicated and in all structured programs that component is a basic requirement, but in private agreement and un-structured cooperation, it might be left out. Normally, while this is a critical point for the industrial partner, there is no conflict or problem with the academic partner. Problems may arise, if that section is not part of the project and is later required by the industrial partner, where the academic partner incurs additional costs not envisaged before.

Direct Economic Aspects

Product development and increased sales are not of any direct concern to the Academy. However, as a partner and probably co-owner of the technology leading to these economic aspects, the Academy is concerned, as it may share liability without sharing the control.

As mentioned above, Collaborative Research is an agreement between unequal partners. This is by far more evident in product development and sales, where the Academy has normally no control and even if it wanted to control issue, has very little experience to allow it to manage the situation. The industrial partner would normally not want any involvement of the Academy in the development and certainly not in the sales. The Academy normally has very little experience in the relevant markets, while the Industry has a very good understanding

---

[31] That is true when the main issue is the utilization of the technology. In start-up companies and sometimes also in larger companies, the IP is used for raising funds, and then title ownership is the main goal.

of the markets, and also has access to the marketing resources and infrastructure. However, as a partner and co-owner of the technology, the Academy may share liability with the Industry, regarding actions taken by the industrial partner out of the control of the Academy, and out of its experience. The Academy would like to see not only indemnification from all liability for actions taken by the Industry, but even more so, would put the entire responsibility for the product development and approval (for example, regulatory and standardization) on the industrial partner. The Academy would normally also try and exempt itself from liability due to infringements of patent rights, claiming to lack the ability to perform the patenting scrutiny necessary to evaluate the risk involved, and ways to circumnavigate existing patents. It would, therefore, expect the industrial partner to manage these issues at its responsibility.

Box 11.2: SRJV–IP Management

> In a SRJV, the Academy asked that the by-laws exempt it from stating that it has checked that the new knowledge developed does not infringe existing patents. The Academy claimed not to have the tools, experience, skills or even the aptitude to do this task. In the resulting argument, some industrial members claim that they do not do that check themselves, even if they suspect that they may be infringing, or especially, if they suspect that. Such a check would either prevent them from acting, or later if sued in court, to triple damages. Others claimed to leave the checks to the patent office. They tend to apply for a patent and let the patent office check. The Academy concluded that this was too complicated and asked to be excused, leaving the right for the industrial members interested in utilizing the technology according to their strategies.

This point of view (expanded in Section "The Academic Point of View") will seem strange to industrial firms normally involved in cooperation with other industrial firms and used to the sharing of the responsibility in a more equal way. However, the industrial partner needs to keep in mind that he is dealing with an un-equal partner, who cannot take the shared responsibility and who may prefer to lose the entire project than enter into an adventure, the potential profit not playing any role at all.

Box 11.3: SRJV-Liability

Such cases, often occur for example in Magnet projects where in the by-laws of the association formed, the section for indemnification is phrased, so that the responsibility for all usage lies with the user of the technology and not with the inventors. It is normally agreed to so, without objection from all partners. However, when the Academy objects to taking responsibility for negligence in that area, there is often disagreement between the Industry and the Academy. The Academy claims that the researchers cannot control all the business or the IP issues of an invention, and would therefore, expect the firms not to take the knowledge as clear and clean, but check it at its *purest form* even before checking the specific utilization of the products and processes, they intend to do. That is a problematic issue and the debates that follow are often very *spirited*. The outcome is often a compromise that can be reached, as the research in these projects is normally generic enough to require much further research and development. As the usage of academic knowledge requires a license, the Academy covers its interests via that secondary agreement.

Licensing Aspects

Another influential and a potential pitfall regarding economic benefits, is the cost of the licensing agreement. Often, due to the generic or basic character of the research, it is very hard to estimate the direct benefit and therefore, the *correct* royalty percentage to the Academy. One must bear in mind that this, is in any case, a commercial issue and not exact science, and therefore, rather flexible. Assuming that the ownership controversy is solved and that the Academy will provide the Industry with a licensing agreement—exclusive to the specific partner—there are licensing aspects that need to be taken into account. This pitfall can be solved with some effort by pre-defining a mechanism for deciding the costs/prices of different options. A clear path towards resolving the issue when it is clear, is best. A rigid definition—the royalties will be in the amount XX and so forth—will encourage in some cases, the partners to try and avoid the situation, and may lead to losing the technology, or discord, and perhaps legal action among members. A clouded definition will lead to uncertainty and to hiding information or lack of cooperation. A balance should be found so that each member understands the process and knows it has a good chance of fair resolution when the time comes (see Table 11.1).

Table 11.1: Licensing Parameters

Aspect	Importance	Problem
Royalty Ratio	Can determine the economic benefit of the project–decision point	Very hard to determine at the early stage of the research. Can often be performance dependent.
Exclusivity	Important for the industrial partners' control over the technology	If dependent upon other basic knowledge that already involves other partners.
Sub-licensing	Same	Raises the issues of control and royalty to the Academy, especially when the industrial partner does not want to be dependent upon the Academy approval for such contracts.
Technology Exchange	Can have strategic significance for the firm	Same problem for the Academy as sub-licensing. Same reluctance from the industrial side to be dependent upon the Academy for approval.

Source: Author's own.

Long-term Capabilities

The long-term capabilities are stated here, separately from the strategic aspects, due to the different roles they play in the industrial consideration to participate in projects or not. These are much less important to firms when considering the value of a project, compared to the other strategic issues aforementioned, and to the direct economic considerations. The industrial partner would normally enter into the collaborative research project, due to the other considerations mentioned; however, in the long-term, this is potentially the most important consideration.

Collaborative research projects allow the industrial partner and the Academy, to develop relational assets that can be applied in the future for much more crucial projects. The industrial partner should find the right balance between the need to control and direct the research and get very industrially oriented results, and academic research that will involve the creation of long lasting cooperation with the academic institute. In addition to relational assets, cooperation with the Academy can have an education/ training aspect that can also help to create technical capabilities in the firm that will allow it to maintain and further the competitive advantage the project created. This aspect of non-research benefits is very important and will contribute to improving the Technology Transfer for the Industrial partner (Katsoulacos and Ulph, 1998).

Box 11.4: SRJV–Knowledge Transfer

> In magnet projects, the firms require the Academy to annually perform a workshop presenting the academic research to the industrial members on a wide basis. Although these workshops contribute mostly to the control of the Industry over the academic research, they do have an aspect of training. More to the point are rare cases in which the Industry will require one or more researchers to give a basic training in order to allow it to better understand the academic research.

THE IMPACT OF SECTOR AFFILIATION

Sectors with high personal change rate tend to try and limit their long-term liabilities towards the other partners. For example:

1. Confidentiality: Keeping the information received from the other partner more secret than one's own information is difficult once the project is over and the people

involved in it have left the company. There is no one left who knows what information was internal and what came from the partners.
2. Developing the relational assets is more difficult, as the relational assets are also based on personal interaction. Continuation becomes more problematic. The confidence that the information exchanged will be kept confidential is harder to develop and maintain.

Porath in his research (2007) showed that open sectors (for example, electronics and communications) tend to establish a larger consortium, where there are additional problems regarding, establishing confidence or relational assets. The organs of the consortia (for example, committees) are more difficult to maintain. It is therefore important to overcome all these sector-originated problems by special social cohesion activities and maintain regular and more intensive meetings.

Small sectors with limited number of partners which may also have some shared history can create sub-groups within the consortia. Thematic sub-groups are normal and natural, but sub-groups created due to shared history are more problematic and may create a political environment that can hinder the smooth operation of the project. That type of problem is very difficult to overcome, but it can be helped if relatively new people in each organization are representing the organization in the consortium, in order to minimize the historic effect.

The project manager should be aware of sectoral characteristics and the potential dangers they could pose to smooth execution of the project.

SUMMARY

It is easy to be taken in by the prospect of the CR, especially at an early stage. However, caution usually sets in very fast (and faster than usual with a legal adviser). There are potential pitfalls and dangers in the CR in general and the SRJV programs specifically.

Some of the pitfalls can be recognized by the intelligent participants and some, only veterans of earlier SRJVs[32] can recognize. The different pitfalls are summarized, as well as, some suggestions as to how they should be addressed have been provided. The point of view of the Academy and that of the Industry are also introduced, as are short and long-term views. A major recommendation for most pitfalls is to resolve them before the commencement of the work in the SRJV. Resolving them can be done by negotiations, by regulations, and by-laws of the SRJV. But, all had better be resolved before the work, otherwise they may hinder the work or worse create a stalemate situation in which the results cannot be used. Therefore, it is better to solve before there are any results to fight about.

One major pitfall is that of being left out of the SRJV. This theme is taken up in the next chapter.

---

[32]Even if from another SRJV program.

12

Left Out: How to Compensate

Having dealt with the pitfalls of joining a SRJV, what happens when you discover you have been left out of one? Or, if you fail to join one that is being formed or that has already been formed. In this chapter, I will show the potential for compensation for being left out of such a project. Where is such a failure fatal? What to do to minimize the damage? I will also discuss the mimetic effect and the wish to join parameters affecting the will to join and parameters slowing that effect.

When a firm discovers that it is left out of a consortium in its relevant sectors, there are two major possibilities for it. One is of no response to the fact. Funnily enough, in the short term this path may be most beneficial for the firm. Non-involvement in early, generic type research is cheap, both in resources and in the risk to the internal knowledge. The firm that does nothing at this stage, does not loose the focus or the direction of existing projects and will certainly benefit in the short term. The second path of course is to react. The reaction should be studied and should be done very carefully. In small concentrated sectors, such reactions may originate from emotions, but that is seldom wise or economic.

A recent study (Stern and Pozner, 2007) describes the mimetic parameters affecting the reaction of firms, to the information that other firms in their sector have formed RJVs. The study focuses on the parameters affecting the reaction, especially, dealing with the formation of alternative RJVs. While the specific environment researched is different,[33] some of the conclusions (as to the effect of size and market performance on the decision) are interesting. This tops the work of others relating to organizational inertia, the links between size and inertia, and the links to organizational structure, perception, and action. The topic of organizational inertia and organizational change relates to the demands on the organization to transform it and adapt to new circumstances, challenges, and threats in the ever-changing environment in which the organization is active. Its relevance becomes clear when the firm will attempt to analyze the first stages of the environmental conditions preceding or following the RJV/SRJV formation, and their influence on the sector.

The underlying meaning can be seen in the earlier research of Cool, Dierickx, and Jemison (1989), who claimed that the creation of a new organizational entity is interesting and rare, deriving mainly from the firm's lack of organizational capacity to develop new competences quickly. Another aspect relevant to the discussion is the evolution and formation of internal organizational routines (Porath, 2003). Research on this topic deals with the development of internal routines within organizations and is relevant to the actions of the firms following the formation, structure, and performance of an SRJV. Spender (1996) referred to routines as part of the process of knowledge creation, claiming them to be superior to institutional identity in that specific context. Grant (1997) claimed that knowledge application, not knowledge creation, is the main task of the organization. At the same time, he agreed that organizational structure had a strong effect on the basis for creating organizational capabilities. McKelvey (1997), later supported by Vonortas (2002), stipulates that a firm's strategic intent is driven by changes in the institutional and competitive environment. The fact that changes in the environment will affect the firms in similar ways, results in those firms also defining their problems in similar ways (Ahuja, 2000). Sanchez and

---

[33]This is assuming that the RJVs are voluntary and that alternatives can be formed at will. Additionally, it does not deal with other venues for operation.

Mahoney (1996) couple the organizational structure to effective coordination and performance, introducing modularity to the general design.

In direct relevance to our discussion, Barr, Stimpert, and Huff (1992) elaborated on the cognitive aspects of the link between the manager's understanding of environmental conditions and a firm's strategy—they perceived this to be a critical one. Teece (1996) deals with the link to Industry as a drive to affect strategy and introduces the idea that formal, as well as, informal structures prevalent in the Industry, combined with the links the firm has, will determine the options open to the firm, leading to a limited range of action options available. Teece (1996) also mentions the characteristics of technological development and the environmental and technological uncertainty involved.

THE FIRST STAGE OF THE REACTION: AN ANALYSIS

The strategic impact of not participating in an SRJV depends on the sector and its characteristics. The SRJV adds one aspect to the strategic aspects of an RJV, and that is, financial support. While some of the participants can be very large and financially well-off organizations, the financial aspect should not be neglected, as most SRJVs come with financial support, unlike RJVs, where the involvement may be purely strategic. The forthcoming discussion will not go into the territory of analyzing the potential of *rigging* of projects by firms, in order to manage to get as much of the financing as possible. While such phenomena may exist, this is not the place to deal with it. It will suffice to say that, such cases are not considered strategic, and for sure present smaller danger to the firm left out, than the cases of real partnership.

The analysis will focus on the following factors. The SRJV gives a certain advantage to its participants like access to other resources, strategic partnerships, and funds. The first thing to deal with when being left out would be damage analysis that would start with the environmental analysis, assessing the potential dangers. The second would be to decide upon the most important factors to compensate for, and prepare and execute the plan to attain them.

ENVIRONMENTAL ANALYSIS

This analysis will focus on the parameters listed below. The purpose of the analysis among others is to give the managers a perspective that is free of subjective influences, like firm history. This is done to give it a realistic scope of alternatives (Barr, Stimpert, and Huff, 1992).

1. Sector concentration: It has been shown that the concentration level of the sector influences the number of participants (Porath, 2007), which in turn, influences the management ability and the effectiveness of the R&D consortium.
2. Portion of the sector involved in the project and its relative mass to those left out: The larger the contingency left out, the greater the potential of those left out to negate the negative results of non-participation, especially in sectors controlled by standards and joint platforms.
3. Resources totally or almost controlled by the CR group: The critical resources should be evaluated here. Critical resources are unique and not easily replaced, or resources that can be out-sourced. The monopoly on critical resources is one of the most dangerous deprecations of being left out and should not be discarded from the analysis.
4. Rate of Spillover in the specific sector: As some sectors (for example, where there is a high turn-over of employees) where the spillover rate is very high, it is in fact an advantage to be left out.
5. What is the basic purpose of the project: There are many *catch-up* projects that are intended to allow the consortium to develop capabilities that exist elsewhere in the world. Such cases mean that the knowledge is out there

and can be purchased and put to use, or that another partnership may be formed. When the project is intended for the development of completely novel technology that does not exist anywhere else, the risk of non-participation is higher, but so is the risk of failure. The failure may be not just limited to technological issues but also to market failure.

HOW TO GET THE DATA WITHOUT PARTICIPATING?

Strangely enough, this is not just a methodical question, but also a cultural question. In business cultures, where everyone knows everyone, mobility of workers between different employers is high and therefore, the Spillover rate is equally high. However, this is not a problem as even in closed cultural environments, the ability to learn what is going on is not a remote possibility. The key to learning what is going on, even if not how it is done, is via the obligations of the sponsoring authority. The authorities tend to try and support the confidentiality of the participants that contradicts the transparency principal, which is becoming more and more important to authorities in the world. Therefore, while details are always protected, the broad lines of the activity will often be in the open world, and clever industrial intelligence will be useful in collecting and analyzing the data. One of the most obvious ways to find out what is going on and in more details than the authority publication, would be through the publishing partner, the Academy. The Academy, even if delayed or censored, will publish some of the research results and that information will allow the firm left out to know who is doing what. These two questions: "Who is performing the work?"—and—"What is this person doing?", are the most important questions, as they identify the people or the sources of the information for future work. Often the research results may be acquired, directly or indirectly, from the Academy and that is the basis for the technology and for future development. The ability to acquire the technology depends on the regulations of the specific consortium and the program under which it runs. This may seem at times to be very strict and solid. However, since the governing authority wants the Industry to be able to use it, there is usually an escape route, which maybe long and difficult.[34]

In any case, since the license, what the industrial members will get from the Academy is non exclusive (as they all should have the ability to get it), and in most cases, it is possible for external firms to get the license. Getting the knowledge would in some cases be also possible without licensing and that would be in the case of publications. However, all this effort is consuming both time and mental faculties from the firm's technological leaders and other departments (like the legal department). This therefore explains the effort to retain the membership even during hard times.

BENEFITS OF STANDARDIZATION

When firms in a consortium make an extra effort, they ensure that their work is not wasted by trying to get it standardized. This can help firms from the outside as their work is now acknowledged as a standard by a standardization body or committee. Firms that have been in and left, or those who considered getting in but avoided the move, are in a good position to access the developers of the standard and employ them for themselves. While the standard is open to all for use, the developers benefit from two main advantages: they are the first to know and understand it, and they are probably more advanced in product development under the standard. For external firms, the second advantage is hard to overcome, as for the rest of the competition, access to deep understanding is theirs to buy. They *know* who the developers are, and they can hire them as workers or consultants and get the

---

[34]The Israeli Magnet Program would confine the ability of licensing the academic invention in a Magnet project to the firms participating. However as this is a national program, there is a route for external firms to acquire the knowledge, albeit with the permission of the current members.

knowledge transferred from them. One could call that move: intended Spillover. While this may contradict confidentiality agreements the consultant or former employees have signed, but these could be difficult to prove and enforce. A consultant that has developed something based on their skill once can do it again, if the skills are not lost. The recruiting firms can cut the advantage of understanding and working according to the standards, when by avoiding membership they did not partake in the risks of developing the standard and the effort to get it approved.

RETIRING FROM THE CONSORTIUM

The regulations expressed in the by-laws would tend to assure that the departure of a partner in the middle of the project does not hurt the success chances of the whole project. The regulations would tend to make sure that:

1. The project work will not be disrupted and will continue. This means that care needs to be taken, in order to find a replacement for the part that the leaving party used to supply within the work program. This includes financial issues like recovery of funds from the leaving partner, transfer of funds for new partners, and so on.
2. The knowledge brought in by the leaving partner and the knowledge that partner has developed, would still be available to the other partners even after the departure. These would include obligations to grant access to the two types of knowledge that would last beyond the partner's tenure within the project.

These factors would make leaving the SRJV a little complicated. The partners leaving may find that they have both financial and IPR obligations, even if they no longer participate in the project. If a partner is leaving because of financial problems, these continuing obligations could be very problematic. Even leaving due to a change in focus is problematic, as the partner is obliged to take care, and allow access rights to IP it no longer views as located within the focus of its strategy. Getting rid of the IP under these conditions with the attached obligations is difficult. So leaving an SRJV in the middle of the work is not easy.

There are several steps to be taken both at the early stage and the later stages.

1. Early Stage:

    a) When deciding to join in the SRJV, explore the options for leaving later—

       (i) What would happen if you wanted to leave in the middle: Reduce your obligation to a minimum and decide what knowledge you will introduce, according to that criteria.
       (ii) Who may take your place if you leave: The knowledge you leave behind would become available to them. Consider that your replacement would be someone with similar capabilities and therefore, probably a competitor.
       (iii) What would happen if your partners decided to leave: Explore ways in which you can reduce your dependence on them and their knowledge. One has to think about what can be done to assure, that the knowledge you need is available for you.

    b) During the life of the project, keep your awareness at a high level for any signs of change of strategy in your partners. Beware of increasing your dependence on the availability of their technology.
    c) Try to make sure that as each part of the knowledge development is complete, the deliverables are kept in a place to which you have access all the time like a central database, central deliverables repository, and

so on. Maintain your own copies whenever possible and make sure your people are familiar with the non-tacit knowledge, as well as, with the tacit knowledge. This will decrease your dependence on the other partners at a later stage.

2. Later Stage:

   a) This is the stage when you want to leave to try and mitigate your future responsibilities. First, check what your obligations are, since usually this stage will happen sometime after the SRJV commencement, and therefore, the people who formed the SRJV are no longer employed by the partners. That would mean that most of them would not know what your obligations are and may use logic or experience from other SRJV programs (without checking). If you had good people in the formation stage, you will find that your real obligations are reduced, compared to, what the partners expect.
   b) If you are leaving due to financial considerations, you may find that it is cheaper to stay in and negotiate a reduction in your obligations, than to leave. If the reason is strategic, please consider the following:

      (i) You can transfer some of the knowledge and related obligations to another partner in the SRJV. This is normally easily done, as the knowledge and its accessibility stay the same for the other partners.
      (ii) You can transfer the knowledge to the funding authority. This is even better, as it reduces the claims the other partners may have on you, and demonstrate that you were acting in a legal way and conforming to the SRJV program regulations.

(iii) You can package the knowledge and deliver it to the repository with the express agreement of the partners freeing you from all future obligations. It is better to supply training and documentation at this stage and leave no obligation open for the future, where you may lack the personnel and infrastructure to supply them, due to internal changes.

(iv) Never ever leave, without closing your future obligations, specifically with the partners. You need to remember that both the partners and the funding authority have an interest in having you still bound to supply them with more reporting training and so on. Your interest is in defining the terms of your release from all future obligations.

STRATEGY

Being left out is a strategic situation. Understanding the actions to be taken requires an analysis, as aforementioned. Among the main issues of the analysis, the basic question is—why were you left out? The CR is regarded as a strategic alliance, therefore, it is clear that this activity is aimed against those not participating in it—the basic question in strategic alliances being: Against whom?

So, if you were left out, it is probably against you, While business is very personal, this is probably not the case here, as you are a part of the group, the effort is made against. This would also mean that you are not alone, and that you can find a second group that can also join forces.

The governing authority would normally not react favorably to funding two competing projects. It would however, be in a position to allow you some access to the knowledge, or to try and find, some compensation for leaving you out. The group that is left out has to come together and see what can be done. A joint effort is normally more powerful, but the goal has to be clear.

The following are the steps that need to be taken:

1. The first logical step would seem to find others in the same position and form a counter alliance. That however is not always possible, and in most cases, as it would not be funded from external sources, it would be very costly for the participants. What should you do next?
2. You should then identify and define the risk for you and the group that you have formed. You need to be able to define the factors to compensate for. The idea of the counter measures is to find the way to compensate for these.

It is important to recall that the measures taken by the research consortium group are for research and could still fail to reach the required goal. The definition of the factors for compensation should take this point into account. This will mean that the external group has to monitor the advancement of the research consortium and be aware of breakthroughs and delays/failures.

TYPES OF FACTORS

Technological Breakthrough

Whether it is a major breakthrough or a minor one, this falls under the need to acquire the technology and access it. The value of the technology should be estimated, and a plan for acquiring it, made and executed. The need to calculate the value comes from the need to be able to assess the financial/economic reasoning of acquiring the technology.

Box 12.1: Spillover Legend

> In ancient times, the production of mirrors was a heavily guarded secret in Europe. In Venice, death was the penalty for transferring that knowledge to outsiders. When the knowledge finally leaked out, several mirror makers who immigrated to other countries, like France, were indeed, killed as punishment.

Remediation steps for the technological breakthrough:

1. The first step would be the identification of the sources for the knowledge and estimation of the probability of acquiring it from them.
2. The second step would be the formation of a detailed plan for performing the task, starting obviously with the most promising candidate. The start with this candidate is again from the economic perspective, and the most promising source would be the cheapest in the long run.

Failure of the Technology to Perform

This is an important aspect of consortia work that is not known well enough. The idea of sponsoring cooperative research and fostering breakthroughs includes the understanding that such efforts can fail. It is more often that technologies would fail, than succeed. Since the effort in technology forming is bigger than in product development, the failure is also more costly and firms tend to avoid it. Funding by the government authority is aimed at, among other things to reduce the risk of co-financing (Luukkonen, 1998, 2000). That point would lead us to the understanding that from time to time, projects performed with the specific consortium would show that the technology fails. There is a possibility that it can be fixed, corrected, and otherwise overcome. Then, it comes under the above mentioned category: Technological Breakthrough. But there are cases when it loses its appeal. It is important for the external firms to know that. The internal firms would like to keep it a secret for two reasons. One, because they may have some other interests involved and would not want the failed technology to be known as a failure, as it could kill earlier products on the market. Two, as they would like the competition not to know that, in order to, make the competition waste time, effort, and funds in pursuing a line of action that they (the internal firms) know is useless, or second best. It can be a very small failure. It can be that a firm would test its own algorithm against a new one coming up, and find that the new algorithm is both faster and more efficient (for example, rate of errors, resources required). If this is published, the existing firm products would be eliminated from the market. Similarly, it can be information regarding the efficacy of a drug under development that could ruin existing drugs on the market.

It is important that you combine forces with the other firms that have been left out, to execute the steps that have been discussed. You need to plan and get the information regarding the actions in the SRJV and its progress regarding the research. This will allow you to know if the technology, has failed or succeeded, and therefore, how to act.

SUMMARY

Being left out of a SRJV, especially in small sectors can be seen as a strategically difficult situation. When in such position, one must consider that the alliance was formed against oneself, and take the steps to compensate for this situation. There are several ways to do so and it is important to try and utilize that condition, for the advantage of the firm left out. In all potential avenues open for the firm, information and the correct analysis of the situation is paramount for all actions to be taken later on. The creation of good information gathering and knowing what is really going on in the SRJV is the key. Based on that information one can decide whether the new technologies are worth having, and from whom, or if it is best to stay apart.

13

The Future of Collaborative Research

Since the late 1990s, there is a growing awareness that Intellectual Capital (IC) is a most important asstet to a firm. IC is *the ability to translate knowledge to financial or other pre-defined targets*. This awareness has also reached the national level in understanding that the economic development of nations and regions is dependent on the IC ability, and on that scale, this ability is dependent upon the capability to translate the knowledge created in the Academy into industrial technology and products. The most famous step taken is the Barcelona Declaration of the EU. The Barcelona Declaration admitted that the US has a strategic advantage over the EU, in the processes, legislation, and industrial–academic culture, allowing it to better use the research potential in the US universities and research centers. In light of that, the EU has declared two main measurable goals to be reached by 2010. The EU should increase its investment in R&D up to three percent of the EU GDP, and 2/3rds of that should come from the private sector. The Barcelona Declaration stating the two parameters had left it to the commission to define the way and the necessary measures to reach that goal.

Such measures can be seen in different but interrelated fields:

1. The EU has increased its funding for research via the commission operated programs (for example, increase in the Framework Program 6 budget).

2. Future programs will be even larger, demanding the increase of the national contribution to the commission budget.
3. Specific programs have been created to combat Brain–Drain, especially towards the US, combined with researcher promoting programs (mobility priority in Framework Program 6—especially the sub programs: IRG, OIF, RTN, and EST).
4. The EU is seeking to increase cooperation with other regions of the world like Latin America, China, and India.

Current trends in collaborative research need to be analyzed in the context of the on-going process related to the role of the research institutes and more specifically, the universities in the world. In 1999, the Israeli Academy formed a review committee, divided into three sub-committees, to analyze the future of the research universities and one of which deals with the interaction between the Academy and the Industry. A similar debate is going on in Europe (taking ERA further), about the role of universities and their contribution to the furthering of the EU, as a Knowledge Based Society. The universities in the EU are also considered to be a major force for economic development (EU COM 58, 2003). The EU is facing the following issues:

1. The need to meet the ever increasing demand for higher education.
2. Maintain and promote scientific and technological excellence.
3. Contribute towards the establishment of the EU as Knowledge Based Society.

The EU (COM 58, 2003) recognizes the problems the EU universities face in the challenging modern world—such as increased demand for higher education, internationalization of education and research, developing effective and close cooperation with the Industry, the emergence of new needs in the forms of new scientific fields, and multi-disciplinary research. However, at the same time the EU recognizes the need to maintain the academic nature and independence of the universities, and to provide them with a stable and continuing source of funding. When discussing the imminent changes in the university scene in the EU, a potential view into the future may be offered by the experience in the Israeli higher education arena. There are many similarities between Israel and the EU in the academic arena, but Israel has its own unique characteristics which must be considered when looking in this sphere. With the increased pressure on universities (EU, 2003) and on the Industry to increase the revenues resulting via TT from basic research, more CR programs and different schemes will be seen.

It is to be expected that not only more CRs (expressed via SRJV programs) but different variations of the same—more adapted to specific needs and more localized—will be seen. However, the CR, the SRJV form, or others, will not exist by itself. The growing trend for more education and training for professional TT officers, combined with regulating the profession (ProTon–mandate) will be accompanied by basic TT education for Academics. The conversion of Research Universities into Research Institutes has a potential risk. Once the Academy via the TT unit becomes involved in CR with the Industry, what will the role of the RI be? Will one form replace the other? What will remain?

However, this is not the place to review the history of the Universities in Europe, since the Middle Ages. They have long been towers preserving knowledge, education, and therefore in some aspects, freedom. Dealing with technological sciences, as well as, Social Sciences and Humanities, they present a complete version of the world. However, the enhanced focus on their future is limited to technological sciences almost exclusively (Bio-Ethics may be a special case), thus reducing somewhat, our understanding of the importance of the university in society into one single plain. Universities are there not just for technological development, but for a world fighting for social value, new definitions of human rights, privacy, and so on. It becomes important therefore, that these issues are pursued and not neglected. One important aspect for universities has been training of the future scientists. This role cannot be neglected and, in fact, in view of the perspective of a Knowledge Based Society, it is even more important today, and will grow in importance in the future.

The need for collaborative research is becoming more and more evident in the on-going discussion about the role of the universities, and in the EU, there are also discussions regarding the large national research centers (in the eastern countries, the national academies are also undergoing a similar transformation). However, in the attempts to forward that activity, one important fact is ignored. The move towards collaborative research is not a step, it is a process, and if encouraged correctly—both on the industrial side for demand, and the Academy (both the institutes and the researchers) for supply—it will grow in time,(as can be clearly seen from Box 13.1 and Figure 13.1).

Box 13.1: SRJV–Repeatability of Participation

> In a research university in Israel, a survey has been made to see how many of the professors involved in collaborative research (in EU Framework Programs) have been involved in more than one project. It appears that once a researcher has been involved in a preparation of at least one proposal, he will attempt again. Only after successive failures to win with different coordinators, will there be an evident withdrawal from the attempts. It is normally those who never try that are reluctant to make the first attempt.

Figure 13.1: Increased CR

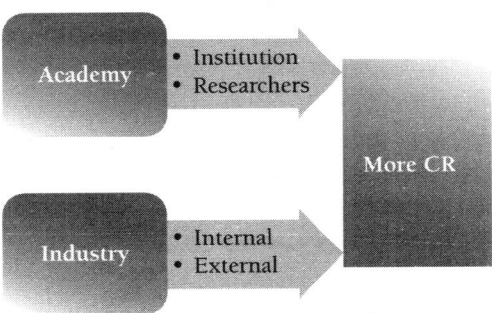

Source: Author.

There is an on-going controversy regarding the impact of applied research on the level of the basic research performed by the academicians (Thursby et al., 2005). The main point to note is that the researchers can differentiate between research performed with, and for the Industry and the basic research they are doing within the Academy. It is important to remember that the current academic system trains the researchers to perform basic research, but leaves applied research to sort of evolve by itself. This approach creates an imbalance in the effort required by the researcher, in order to get involved in applied research, and requires in turn, big incentives to take that step. It also lies at the back of the approach that the applied research is inferior to basic research (among other reasons).

SUMMARY

This chapter discussed the evolution of collaborative research and its future. Two trends seem to converge. With the increased importance of knowledge-based economic sectors, the authorities are trying to increase the knowledge flow from the Academy to the Industry. The second is the need for having a better account for public spending. The drive towards more and more research, and the need to justify public spending, especially national spending on research, is creating a drive to link the public expenditure on research to economic growth. The surest way seems to be to link the Academy to the Industry. That trend will increase in intensity. It is perhaps a point to remember that research; basic research, that is, not application oriented, contributed most of the greatest inventions and technologies, and should not be neglected in favor of development.

The intensity of the linkage will increase on regional-national and super-national levels, and therefore, understanding the factors behind the programs of Collaborative Research is important.

14

How to Build a Successful Collaborative Research Program

GENERAL

The topic of this chapter is very ambitious; therefore, some clarification is required so expectations would be realistic. This chapter will not give the full-blown details of the best practice in a leading collaborative research program. It will not supply a fully developed, all encompassing, general yet localized program—were such a thing possible. It will present several types of programs and give the basic outlines for each. The full-blown development is left for the reader to fill in, taking into account localized legal and cultural aspects. The types of program to be discussed would be the following: Basic to Applied Research (BAR), Validation and Technology Transfer (VATT), and Non-Generic Cooperation (NGC).

The chapter will begin with the basics for planning a research program and will proceed from there to the three program examples. The discussion will include some of the tools for planning and affecting, and provide examples of their use.

THE RATIONALE

The basic step before any planning or designing is to check the rationale behind the program. This chapter will assist in planning the programs in order to fit strategically, the aims and long-term goals of the authority executing the plan. It is useless to simply copy a program from another authority or another region/country, as regions vary significantly in their economic-social parameters, and solutions need to be adapted to these variations. This chapter will set the early stages of preparation and strategic analysis for the program followed by the formulating process, the analysis points, and instruments to be developed with the program. The chapter will end with the launch of the program. However, one should remember the principals mentioned earlier in this book:

1. The industrial needs and fears.
2. The Academic view.
3. The goals set out for the programs.
4. The existing environmental conditions.
5. Combining them all into a comprehensive plan and executing it.

Box 14.1: VC Market

> The Israeli Venture Market is a remarkable case in the development of the innovation sector. In 1989, Israel had virtually no venture capital. There was one bi-national foundation that supported US-Israeli cooperation, several private investors, and a bank that from time to time would invest in a new company. By 2003, the Israeli Venture Capital sector had over 100 registered funds with a raised 10.5 billion USD—as reported by the IVA—this was the Israeli Venture Capital Association. But, can this development be copied for use in other countries today? The fast development in Israel of the VC sector was accompanied by a fast development in the other tools assisting the formation of start-ups (for example, nationally assisted 28 Technology Incubators), and the *bubble* of the 1990s. Israel's temperament of entrepreneurship has created a country, where the term, Small Medium Enterprise would normally refer to a High-Tech Start-Up, and not to a traditionally small firm. These cannot be copied today, and therefore trying to copy the Israeli development of VC would require serious consideration.

ADAPTING EXISTING PROGRAMS

The cheapest solution is to adopt an already adapted successfully running program. When adapting, one follows similar paths to

How to Build a Successful Collaborative Research Program 181

the development of new programs, but the process is both faster and the chances for success are bigger. Figure 14.1 depicts such a chain of adaptation of existing programs that were adapted from one country to another. The figure is done in a simulation of a genealogical map, as it is known which program served as the source for the next. For most programs, the list is not so long or so detailed, but successful programs will be copied. The

Figure 14.1: Competence Centers Genealogical Map

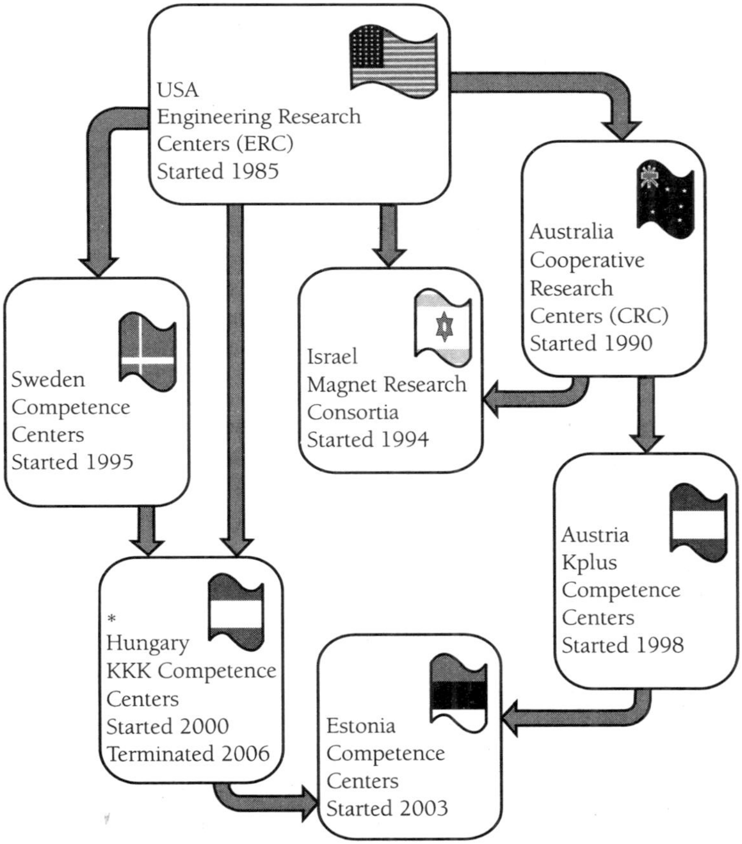

```
                    USA
                    Engineering Research
                    Centers (ERC)
                    Started 1985
         ┌──────────┴──────────┬──────────────┐
         ▼                     ▼              ▼
    Sweden              Israel           Australia
    Competence          Magnet Research  Cooperative
    Centers             Consortia        Research
    Started 1995        Started 1994     Centers (CRC)
                                         Started 1990
                                              │
                                              ▼
                                         Austria
                                         Kplus
                                         Competence
                                         Centers
                                         Started 1998
         │                                    │
         ▼                                    ▼
    *Hungary                             Estonia
    KKK Competence   ─────────────────▶  Competence
    Centers                              Centers
    Started 2000                         Started 2003
    Terminated 2006
```

Source: Adaptation of a figure from the author's PhD thesis.
Note: *Discontinued.

EU Commission has even specified that as a goal in its Open Method of Coordination scheme. The selected successful programs are referred to as *Best Practices* and recommended for copying/adaptation. The idea is that with increasing similarity and homogeneity of the EU, such *Best Practices* should become prevalent all over the EU.

THE FIRST STEP: ANALYZING

Collaborative Research programs do not exist just because they are "nice to have". They exist because they serve at least one (normally more than just one) strategic goal, important to the controlling authority. As adapting a program would necessitate, at least adapting it to the business and legal environment of the recipient, it is important to do the adaptation correctly, so as to maintain the important (providing the desired end result) parts, while adapting/changing/fitting the other parts (supporting parts) of the program.

The first step therefore, would be a strategic assessment of the need for such a program, and defining the need and derived targets appropriately. The strategic assessment would start by identifying the need and the assets, and would therefore, simulate a Strength, Weakness, Opportunity, Threats (SWOT) analysis. The Strength and Weaknesses would allow a strong and precise definition of the need for the program. The Opportunities and Threats would supply the means and assets to be used. In order to better understand the meaning, consider the example given in Box 14.2.

Box 14.2: Regionalism

> Two regions in the same country are considering promoting their industry and improving their competitiveness. One of the regions is located at the heart of the heavy metal industry, with a long tradition of large firms with a strong affiliation to material industry and mechanics. There are also several technical universities, as well as, technical high schools; this is the Mechanical Region (MR). The second region is characterized by High-Tech companies with strong activities in electronics, software, and communications; this is the Electronic Region (ER). Here again, the academic

Contd. Box 14.2

Contd. Box 14.2

> institutes reflect the general industrial tendencies. The two regional governments will develop two different support schemes. The MR government will formulate a plan that will encourage close research between the universities and the Industry, where the Industry will co-finance the research, and will have primary or exclusive rights to the results, in combination with assuring the research students', potential employment in the firms. The ER, on the other hand, will try and promote more loosely connected research of the universities with the Industry, offering the Industry first refusal or similar advantages, in return to a lesser degree of financial participation in the research. But, the ER government will develop support infrastructure and mechanisms for the creation of start-ups and spin-offs resulting from the research. The industrial research partners will be encouraged to invest in the resulting firms, and a regional venture capital support system will be developed, as part of the program.

In the example given in Box 14.2, which has its parallel in real life, the two regions are located in the same country, so as to eliminate all cultural/lingual legal differences. However, with the increasing financial, economic, and legal integration of the EU, such examples can also be given internationally, with similar validity. The SWOT analysis will be based on the questions discussed in the next section, which will form the skeleton for a detailed questionnaire.

SWOT

The main goal of this step is to find the needs and identify the resources applicable to our case. The questions should be divided into the following sections:

1. General

    (a) What is the legal frame work for R&D programs: Laws, regulatory authorities, or budgetary allocations?
    (b) Who among them operates a program and to what end?
    (c) Characteristics of existing programs: Problems to be solved, resources invested, and common practices.

2. Economic

    (a) Characteristics of local industry: Type, human or capital inclined, life cycle of products.
    (b) Involvement of local Industry with Academia: How, where, and at what stage of R&D?
    (c) Local (public and private) investments in R&D: Total investments compared to national investments and other indices.

3. Finance

    (a) Available budgets and their resources.
    (b) Availability of financing organizations in the region.
    (c) The ability of the Industry to participate in co-financing.

4. Academy resources

    (a) Type of expertise and disciplines available in the area;
    (b) Availability of funds to increase the academic infrastructure;
    (c) The capabilities of the private sector research;
    (d) The openness of the Academy towards cooperation with the Industry (for example, cultural barrier depth and traditions in the field of cooperation).

SWOT Drawing

It is important to make sure that the needs are identified correctly. Mis-identification leading to a program designed to fit different needs will not reach the desired results. Shutting down a program will result in loosing Industry–Academy confidence in the authority, SRJV or the CR in general. Once the SWOT has managed to map the different aspects, the general outlines of the program can be drawn. This process has been described in the next section.

The results of the SWOT will serve as the basis for designing measurable attainable goals for the program. One of the major points that the SWOT results should address is the value returned by potential programs compared to the investment in them.

DESIGNING THE PROGRAM

After performing the SWOT, the needs and therefore the goals for a program should be clear, as well as the assets available for utilization, and the assets lacking yet. The program will need to acquire the missing assets, as well as, recruit the existing ones. However, before that is done, the design of a program requires a clear and precise definition of the needs the program will have to address.

NEEDS AND GOALS: DEFINITION

This seemingly trivial step is crucial to the success of the program: the attainment of the goals it sets out to achieve. The SWOT may give clear information regarding problems, but the goals have to be:

1. Defined in clear and quantitative way.
2. The goals should not only have measurable targets but also a time frame to achieve them.
3. The goals should be ambitious, but appear to be realistic—too ambitious will result in difficulties when trying to obtain the resources.

Whenever a decision is made, one of the important factors is to test the design. Use the potential target clients to test the program. Test it over a trial period, combined with evaluation reports of external evaluators, as well as interviews with the participants. All this evaluation needs to be done, in order to determine the efficacy of the program, the level of satisfaction, and the changes required to improve efficacy, efficiency, and attractiveness.

Only after such a period should the program be officially and fully launched. Since the technological world, and all other sectors, is always changing, the programs need to be monitored regularly. The best way to achieve that is relatively easy in SRJVs. This is done by just incorporating the monitoring aspect in the administrative side of the program.

How to fit components to *needs*?

PROGRAM EXAMPLES

In this section, three types of programs will be discussed and presented. These types are characterized by their end goals and participants. The outlines and basic assumptions for each, will be described in the following sections. The types are:

1. Basic to Applied Research (BAR)
2. Validation and Technology Transfer (VATT)
3. Non-Generic Cooperation (NGC).

Basic to Applied Research (BAR)

The BAR type program is intended to use basic capabilities existing in the research community (universities, public research organizations, and private research organizations) to enhance the research capabilities and assist in developing joint sectoral technologies or technology platforms. The research refers to basic research in the research organization (understanding nature and its phenomena), extending into applied research—seeking to use the understanding into manipulations, required by society—and mainly Industry.

Such a program would assume the participation of two kinds of partners; the basic research providers (Academy in various forms), and application oriented organizations, which in technological fields would mean the Industry. While in other fields, different organizations may be the application driven partners (like, for instance, hospitals in medicine, health-care organization in public health area, municipalities in human resources, and tourism), for this discussion, they will be referred to as Academy and Industry.

It would be expected to have as deliverables from BAR programs, a significant increase in the competitive abilities of a specific sector, as well as, the potential for increased economic activity and benefits (which influence the trade balance, job creation, and preservation of employment). Additional deliverables may be expected due to other characteristics of the program (see Box 14.3). Projects under the BAR program would have more measurable and specifically defined deliverables. Such deliverables would serve as part of the evaluation criteria between competing projects proposals, as well as their viability.

In BAR programs, due to their nature and the nature of the partners, two additional aspects or characteristics emerge—the financial support given to the projects in less than 100 percent (due to competition laws and the industrial partner) and the joint work. The latter normally ends short of a final product, this is mainly due to the academic partners, but it also has to do with competition laws. In cases where the research goes all the way to a final product, the support is normally termed as a loan to be returned from the sales of the product/s. In most other cases, the support is a grant.

Box 14.3: BAR

> The EU Framework Program Cooperation projects (the large, as well as the small and medium projects), are examples of BAR projects. Such projects are intended exactly for the aforementioned purposes, while corresponding with the policies and agendas of the EU. The topics of the projects and the priority given to each one are additional aspects to the type of research and the partners in them, but important aspects as they determine the deliverables and the by-laws of the program.

The BAR program is becoming very popular. The Academia seems to be a source for many interesting inventions and the transfer of these inventions to the Industry can result in great economic benefits (EU, 2003, 2006). Some countries such as Italy, Sweden, and Germany have put some effort into changing their systems into creating more collaboration between Industry and Academy, and also to try and help ideas spin-off the Academy and into the industrial–economic world.

It is important to keep in mind that the Academy, by training, is not qualified to make such a move and that the Industry should lead the application orientation in any such venture, if it is to succeed. The capabilities of the program and the projects it supports to achieve real tangible deliverables and economic benefits are dependent on the leadership of the Industry (the application partner). On the other hand, the Industry is more often than not, incapable of understanding that academic research is different by nature from industrial R&D. The expectations of the Industry to have industrial measures and culture of work in the academic research is often the source of many disappointments. That is not to say that academic research is all play and no work, just that it is different by nature. The Industry needs to understand that the academic partners are different from R&D or engineering subcontractors they may normally have. The acceptance by each partner of the other is the result of experience in most cases, and here old partners have the benefit of relational assets.

Validation and Technology Transfer (VATT)

These programs are intended to assist, not the general transfer of knowledge from Academy to Industry, but to do so through very specific and well-defined points. This could be viewed not as linking the Academy to the Industry, but rather a specific lab to a specific R&D department in the Industry.

The purpose here is to go beyond the general research capabilities and potential applications for the future and deal with the specific issue of problem solving. The idea is that the Academy may have the solution to problems the Industry has in its development. For that purpose and as academic knowledge is far from the maturity level, the Industry is required, to have the ability to validate the knowledge (may also require some research and development to make it fit industrial needs) and then transfer it to the Industry. The program here would try and bring together smaller groups than in the BAR programs. The research here would definitely be applied research, where the needs and the difficulties will be defined by the Industry. The role of the Academy is that of a knowledge-provider, with the skills to adapt it to the needs described by the Industry.

The main deliverables would benefit the Industry in developing new products (including processes) and overcoming competitiveness difficulties. The cooperation between the Academy and Industry on a close to the product basis would also demand that the knowledge be delivered to the Industry in a usable format. That would mean that while in the BAR program, dissemination of results would be an acceptable principle, as well as, the protection of the IP. In most VATT programs, the requirement for IP protection would supersede the principle of dissemination.

The financial support in this case again, would be partial and the conditions termed even stronger, towards the preservation of competition fair play. Thus, if the final product is reachable via the VATT program, the funding will be termed as a loan, but if it is left at the technological or proto-type stage, it could be a grant.

It may be advisable for the VATT program to either lay down the regulations and terms for the Technology Transfer, or elsewhere prepare a process for the determination of the conditions and the transfer. On the other hand, it may simply require as a precondition to the funding, a conditional transfer agreement (can be transfer of ownership, or license to use). It is advisable to do so not only to protect the interests of the parties, but also of the funding agency. However, in many cases, the value of the technology is difficult to determine at the start of the project, which would make the preparation of the transfer agreement difficult. A mechanism for determining the conditions is a safer solution.

Box 14.4: VATT

> The Eureka small projects may seem like a good VATT example. They are specifically defined and their outcome in the form of a product is an expected deliverable. The funding schemes however, are localized, in order to fit the legal aspects of each country participating in the projects. In this case, the regulations are complicated by the international aspect. The Eureka program (www.eureka.be) has been a success due to its practical nature and the measurable direct benefit it brings the participants.

Non-generic Cooperation (NGC)

In many countries and regions, there is a mechanism for supporting industrial R&D. The purpose of the mechanism is to encourage the Industry to further the development of new products and processes and, therefore, benefit from the increased competitiveness of the Industry. The programs for such support to the industrial R&D encourage in many cases, and allow in most, the participation of the Academy as a sub-contractor to the Industry for projects. This cooperation is different in nature than the other two described before this—in that the Academy exists solely by the pleasure of the Industry. The Academy brings its benefit to the Industry, but must normally show value for money for the project, as the Industry has to pay, at least, part of the academic research expenses from its own pocket, or exchange it for internal R&D.

The nature of the program and the fact that the Academy is an option, dictates the type and nature of the deliverables, as well as, the characteristic by-laws. The IP protection will supersede complete dissemination and the dissemination may be minimal. The nature of the work would be development with some more general contributions from the Academy, pre-defined and characterized by the Industry. This type of work would probably result in patents or trade secrets, but with very little chance for academic publications. The NGC would be more fitting to research organizations than for universities, where they would probably take a secondary role in the research portfolio of faculty members.

Funding in NGC would almost always be termed as a loan dependent upon success.

Box 14.5: NGC

> The US-Israeli Bi-National Foundation (BIRDF http://www.birdf.com/) projects are such NGC examples. It is an industrial cooperation foundation, where the Academy may participate solely as a sub-contractor to the industrial partners, who must also fund it from their resources. The maximum support is 50 percent of the approved budget, and that is, as a loan to be repaid from sales of the resulting products. The program has been in operation since 1974 and has had numerous projects.

SUMMARY

This chapter demonstrated the formation process of collaborative research programs and three types of such programs were outlined. The structuring of collaborative research programs is a strategic process, which requires the analysis of the environment and the players, as well as, the required results followed by adapting the proposed structure to them.

The three types of programs outlined here were selected with the intent of demonstrating different levels of cooperation between the Academy and Industry and different types of research. Real world examples have been provided for each type.

In every region and country, the structured programs intended for the development of the Industry and the knowledge-based economy are funded from public funds, and they are projects aimed for the benefit of the participants and the region. It is important to identify the deliverables that stem from the type of program, and the deliverables that stem from other goals and purposes, and that are incorporated into the programs by the authority.

15

National Application (India)

This chapter will present a country sample showing a snapshot of the current status and development in the CR field. India will be summarily presented, with some samples and some potential venues for the development of CR programs and activities. It will begin with a description of the current status in research and in Industry, and move to the future.

INDIA: A COUNTRY SAMPLE

The discussion in the previous chapters, with the samples, may still seem to be a bit theoretical. Specific samples may demonstrate some industrial cases, but a country sample will make the picture more vivid.

India has been recognized since the early 2000s as a service center, and more and more services are being outsourced there. Software development has been also a source of many outsourcing efforts. However, India has the Human Resources and the R&D management capabilities, as well as, the scientific infrastructure and personnel to allow it to realize a strong potential in the R&D field. This chapter will present a picture of the potential development that Collaborative R&D between Academy and Industry in India can have on economic development, and how it can have a synergetic effect with the current developments in India and trends in the world.

INDIA: ACADEMIC RESEARCH INFRASTRUCTURE

General

The educational system of India is too large to be fully described in this volume. The focus we are looking for, in this section, is the excellence of the educational system and its ability to perform research and to transfer that research to the Industry. In this section, the leading system will be reviewed and the relations with the Industry be checked as well. For the purpose of developing the Collaborative R&D capabilities and infrastructure, the important factor to check is the quality and presence of leading technological R&D centers on the academic side, as well as, their relations and relational assets with the Industry.

It is important that in addition to, an international level of scientific research quality, the research centers checked should have access/contacts in the Industry, and possess the infrastructure to support Collaborative R&D with the Industry: Legal, administrative, financial, and the right type of encouragement.

Basic Parameters

The following parameters were mentioned previously:

1. **Scientific Quality:** The science produced must be of excellent quality. The resulting technologies developed in the CR will have to lead to world-class quality and competitively enhanced products. Without world-class research competing with other such researches, it would be very difficult to develop world-leading technologies. The Industry will have to develop the products, but the technologies would be very difficult to develop without world-class science. This parameter refers to the quality of the work, as published in international journals, as well as to patents approved in countries, other than India, fulfilling the international parameter. Another aspect of

the same parameter is the level of infrastructure open for usage by the members of the centers. The quality of the human resources is judged by their acceptance in foreign institutes as faculty members and research students.

2. **Legal:** The legal framework allowing for CR and for involvement of the centers (universities, private, and public national centers) in CR with the Industry. It allows the centers, the researchers, the students, and infrastructure in such activities. In our case as the international involvement is an important facet of the activity, it is important to check that the legal framework allows for the involvement of foreign bodies and that the fruits of the activities of such foreign bodies can be utilized by these bodies.

3. **Administrative:** The administrative infrastructure is paramount for a high level of CR activity. Academic researchers are used to having their administrative support, taking care of all the non-scientific aspects. It is important for them to have at least the same level of support for CR as they would have for basic science research. In most cases, the administration in academic institutes is not designed for working with profit organizations. It may require more involvement on the administration side more reporting, including HR capital investment, in addition to the regular R&D reporting. The administration may need involvement of researchers from the industry, as well, as loaning their researchers or students for work in the industry, and treat these aspects as part of the regular activity of the institute. In order to assure a significant volume of CR, the activity needs to become a regular activity of the center and not a special case.

4. **Finance and encouragement:** The financing of CR may be more complex than the finance the research centers are used to, from academic funding sources or foundations. In most cases the research centers are funding their research from single sources (with or without self participating or self financing). In many cases CR would demand at least

an approval by the industrial partner, but may also include a contribution from them. The employment conditions in the research centers and the Industry need to be reconciled and that may demand adjustments in the financial system. Financial reporting may require changes or adaptations to be made to the accounting system (for example, linking overhead expenses to direct expanses, purchases of components or materials to specific projects and not departments and so on). While these types of changes may also be required from the Industry, the industrial system is usually more flexible. The encouragement for the researchers should include some financial compensation, which both the legal framework should allow and the financial system needs to be able to supply. It is important to recall that the scientific credit is normally smaller for CR activity compared to academic research. Financial compensation may not equate the loss in academic production (fewer articles to be published), but it may help compensate by allowing to establish the research infrastructure, equipment and personnel, as well as for the leading researcher.

For the above-mentioned parameters to be applied to the Academy in India, it would require a huge book in itself. In this chapter, we will observe the more readily available information and focus on the results.

INDIA: SCIENTIFIC EXCELLENCE

India has presented the world with leading scientists [DST (1), 2009a] such as Srinivasa Ramanujan, J.C. Bose, and C.V. Raman, among many others.

After Independence, India has placed Science and Technology as a priority that will allow the country to maintain and further the quality of Human Resources, it would need for economic growth. In its ST policy of 2003, it is stated in the Preamble:

In the half century since Independence, India has been committed to the task of promoting the spread of science. The key role of technology as an important element of national development is also well recognized. The Scientific Policy Resolution of 1958 and the Technology Policy Statement of 1983 enunciated the principles on which the growth of science and technology in India has been based over the past several decades. These policies have emphasized self-reliance, as also sustainable and equitable development.

That Commitment has not slacked over the years. In his 2003 Policy opening words (ST Policy, 2003) the Honorable Dr Manmohan Singh, Prime Minister of India states:

We take satisfaction from the fact that over 100 global companies have come to India to set up R&D Centres, affirming the intellectual capital of our scientific and engineering community. Science must grapple with the key challenges facing the country today. These include the pressures of increasing population, greater health risks, changing demographics, degraded natural resources, and dwindling farmlands. We need new science and technologies, new priorities and new paradigms to address these fundamental challenges.

These words indicate the recognition of changes in the world, and the dedication to a solution that is internal based.

The Indian academic system described in the next section is supported by a long tradition of researchers who have graduated from it, and have gone on to more advanced degrees around the world; locally the graduates have been incorporated into a system that has been famous for its high level of education (Friedman, 2006). In his book, Friedman states that the establishment of the Indian Institutes of Technology in the 1950s, according to the vision of the then Prime Minister Pandit Jawaharlal Nehru has led to the development of scientific and engineering based excellence. He mentions that since 1953, over 25,000 graduates have settled in the USA. He further states that there is a claim that it is more difficult to get accepted into one of these institutes, than into MIT.

The ST policy (2003) further states the readiness to enact and promote actions that will aid and foster further R&D in India:

To encourage research and innovation in areas of relevance for the economy and society, particularly by promoting close and productive interaction between private and public institutions in science and technology. Sectors such as agriculture (particularly soil and water management, human and animal nutrition, fisheries), water, health, education, industry, energy including renewable energy, communication and transportation would be accorded highest priority. Key leverage technologies such as information technology, biotechnology and materials science and technology would be given special importance.

To substantially strengthen enabling mechanisms that relate to technology development, evaluation, absorption and upgradation from concept to utilization.

To establish an Intellectual Property Rights (IPR) regime which maximizes the incentives for the generation and protection of intellectual property by all types of inventors. The regime would also provide a strong, supportive and comprehensive policy environment for speedy and effective domestic commercialization of such inventions so as to be maximal in the public interest.

In the strategic chapter of the policy (ST policy, 2003), it is stated that the governmental ministries and departments will support the policy by programs, as will the states. An aim of the policy, as stated in the chapters of the Science and Technology Policy (ST policy, 2003), is to raise the level of R&D investment (government and private sector) to a level of 2 percent of GDP, by the end of the tenth plan.

In summary, the policy recognizes the importance of R&D, allocates the responsibilities, and mentions the tools, and measurable goals for fulfillment.

RESEARCH AND EDUCATION SYSTEM

The system today, according to the DST [DST (1), 2009b], has about 200 national laboratories performing national research together with Central Sector institutes (1,300). There are also 162 universities, 32 institutions deemed as universities, and 10 national institutes. They provide India with over 200,000 graduates that swell its research, engineering, and medicinal ranks. In

1990, the S&T human resources in India were estimated to be around four million.

The Indian research support system is supported by the government (see the next section on "India Research Investment"). The Industry is mainly contributing to its own research. The Academy and national research organization are working along two main avenues. On the one hand, the Academy being encouraged to excel in research, to cooperate [DST (1), 2009a] internationally, is concentrating on basic non-directed research and on the other hand, the government mindful of its responsibility to promote research in directions that will allow the local Industry to be competitive in the world, is directing research and efforts towards such areas. For example, the Nano Mission launched in May 2007, with an allocation of Rs 1,000 crore for, five years, [DST (3), 2009c], or others such as the Solar Energy Initiative or the Water Technology Initiative. The annual report of the Department of Science and Technology [DST (2), 2009b] mentions some 495 science and engineering projects, with the total cost of 13188.7 lakhs, as approved during 2007 for research.

INDIA: RESEARCH INVESTMENT

During 1993–1994, the governmental share of R&D was 74 percent of the total R&D [DST (1), 2009a]. According to the ERAWATCH (2009) report, as late as 2007, India R&D expenditure was 1.14 percent of the GDP. In 2005, it was about 5.5 billion Euros, which in PPP terms is about 24 billion Euros. That places India behind China (81 billion), but before Brazil and South Africa. The same report states that in scientific output measured in research publications, India is 13 from 146 countries around the world. Since then, however, the private sector has been very actively collecting research opportunities from around the world. That should change the balance in areas such as software development, services, and so on. However in the physical sciences, the government remains the main investor in R&D.

The central government operates the following departments in S&T (see Figure 15.1):

1. Department of Science and Technology (DST)
2. Department of Scientific and Industrial Research (DSIR)
3. Department of Atomic Energy (DAE)
4. Department of Space (DoS)
5. Department of Biotechnology (DBT)
6. Department of Ocean Development (DOD)

Figure 15.1: Central Government Departments Dealing with Research

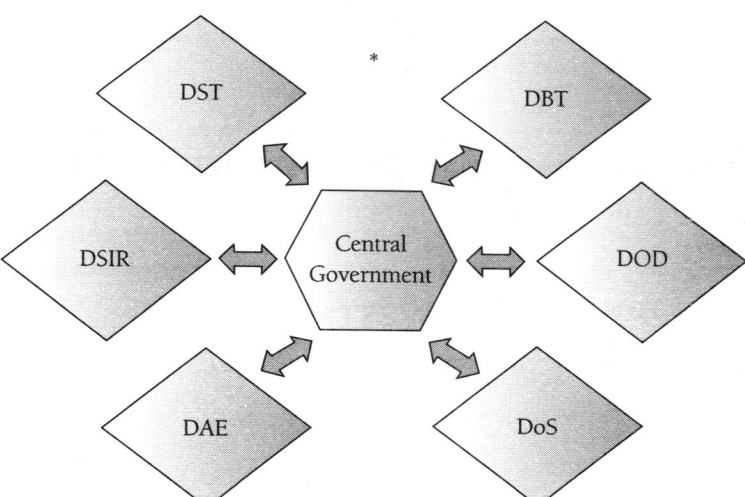

Source: Author's own.
Note: *Other departments dealing with agriculture, defence, and earth sciences were deemed less relevant for civilian industrial cooperation and were, therefore, not included in the list and drawing.

DST is responsible for S&T policy and programs for the national goals. It has the tools for financing the S&T activities. DSIR operates the Council of Scientific and Industrial Research (CSIR), and is responsible for encouragement of R&D in Industry, Technology Transfer, and technological self-reliance.

According to Krishna (2009), it seems that most of the R&D in India has been performed in the public sector, however, the private sector too is increasing its investment. Data updated on November 21st, 2008.

> While bulk of research is performed under the auspices of government science agencies and its constituent laboratories, private sector accounts for approximately quarter of GERD in terms if R&D expenditures. The private sector has come into sharp focus in the last 3-5 years as India has been a major destination of Foreign Direct Investment and an attractive knowledge based location for Transnational Corporations such as Microsoft, General Electric among others. 250 global firms (most of which are the fortune 500 companies) have set up their R&D centers/laboratories and units in Hyderabad, Bangalore, Delhi, Gurgaon, Pune and Noida. As mentioned in earlier section 8.4.2 about 2.3 billion US$ has been spent by foreign R&D centers in India in 2006.

INDIA: INDUSTRY-ACADEMY COOPERATION

Research performed in the Indian Industry consists of a large number of foreign companies investing mostly in development work in the country (see Dr Manmohan Singh's speech), in addition to the internal R&D companies. The opening, in 1991, of the Indian markets to foreign investment, and reduction of Red Tape has allowed further growth. According to Friedman (2006), it is still a question as to what India intends to make of its potential, regarding future developments. The capabilities, the infrastructure, and also, more and more experience is there.

In the model in which Academy research results are commercialized centrally by CSIR (Krishna, 2009), the direction is from top (government agency) to down (the Industry representing the market). While such centralization allows for more efficiency and probably reduced costs (as the duplication of costs is eliminated) one must question the marketing relevance of one central entity in commercialization of all research results.

In that model, the single agency for the entire public research system—for significant part of it—can also be a limiting factor regarding innovation. The agency could have a natural affinity to promote technologies developed by its own centers over others. In countries where each institute or group of institutes have their own administrative/commercializing unit, this helps create the following capabilities within that institute:

1. Direct link with the Industry.
2. Familiarization with Industry needs.
3. Adaptability to changing needs derived from fast changing market conditions.

The above listed capabilities allow for competing technologies to develop in partnership with industrial partners, and thus to compete in the local market, an early trial before entering the international markets competition. The above also allows the creation of a plethora of ideas to be presented to the Industry, allowing the Industry to select which will be further developed, based on market understanding and potential. In today's fast changing market conditions, this will create a marketing advantage for Indian Industry.

While this situation will be more expansive, as the number of such units—the public purse will need to support—will increase, the potential benefit cannot be ignored. Another side benefit from a large number of such units will be the creation of a new profession, the Technology Transfer Officer, who with time will also migrate to the Industry and will help promote the R&D support activities that India proposes. Plus with time, as is seen more and more around the world, these units potentially will become self-sufficient economically, and even profitable, for the benefit of their holding institutions.

INDIA: FUTURE DEVELOPMENT POSSIBILITIES

In the sections discussed in this chapter, the case of India has been briefly summarized. It is a simple case where in fact all the necessary ingredients are there: the excellence both in Industry and Academy to perform research, knowledge about the market, government recognition of the importance of R&D for the future and its willingness to support, the experience in performing R&D both in Industry and in Academy, and finally the basis for investment.

All that is left to see are the tools that exist for the cooperation and what can be done to improve the results.

There are about 20 research associations of different sectors such as Automotive and Wool (Krishna, 2009), which together with the few R&D related consortia such as Biotechnology, have invested in the 1990s an average of about 1.1 million Euros. The Industry investment in the Magnet Program projects in the same period in Israel, was at least double of that (not counting the government support). However, if that is the main R&D cooperation between Industry and Academy, what about the commercialization results of the public R&D?

When the system allows for a central agency to commercialize the significant bulk of research results obtained by the public research infrastructure (Krishna, 2009), that agency, for instance, the Council for Scientific and Industrial Research (CSIR), operates under DSIR, and aims to promote the industrial competitiveness, and is also in charge of Industry–Academy cooperation and commercialization of results. CSIR has 38 laboratories and institutes and 39 outreach centers. DSIR, with CSIR, is a model department for several government schemes for Technology Transfer.

In this book, the advantages of CR as a method for both development of relevant technologies and development in a relevant way of technologies, for industrial use on the one hand and on the other hand, has been advocated as the leading tool for Technology Transfer. The "fine tuning" proposed here, requires direct contact and maximum flexibility.

While India shows many success stories of technologies been transferred from the research organizations to the Industry, there seems to be a place for CR as a tool for both, enhanced Technology Transfer and an increase in the relative weight of Industry investment in R&D, as part of the GDP.

A further study into the economic benefit of the university/research institute unit for commercialization is recommended.

It may be felt that extending this activity beyond the agency would improve the current rate of cooperation and Technology Transfer.

Furthermore, it would seem that state-wide, or, with or without central government support, programs that would encourage cooperation in research between Industry and Academy have been described in the previous chapters. These programs should allow the market to direct them by allowing the Industry to suggest the necessary topics and direct the required public research performers towards the results required by the Industry. The finance decisions should be governed by market potential. The market potential would be the ability of the industrial partners to bring the results to the market, and the potential revenues to the Industry that these actions would bring. It is important to allow the Industry to lead the topics, but it is important that the state govern and monitor the project financed, in order to make sure, it is been utilized in the correct way.

CR programs can be established with a local vision. State management is important as it allows medium-size and small companies to benefit by reducing travel expenses and facilitating better direct contact. The Central government may also form supplement programs (for example, to assist in IP training for public research faculty members) that allows the creation of networks of CR program managers to share practices, experiences, and successful solutions.

The state oriented CR programs may also be tailored to fit the specific infrastructure, both in Industry and in research organizations in the specific states. Areas mostly rural and with strong agricultural basis may concentrate more on the food industry, while others may benefit from the presence of a strong biotechnology industry. Such state-wide programs have been successful in India. The Software Technology Parks of India (STPI) program, which started as a state program in Karnataka, and was followed by other state governments is such a success case. Its has supported IT industries that have among other things, resulted in over 6,000 software export companies under the STP1 umbrella (Krishna, 2009).

These CR programs would require the public research sector to develop the commercialization units with their infrastructure and human resources. These will also help increase the size of Industry cooperative-ready researches, in the public research sector.

SUMMARY

This chapter took a brief look at a sample country—India, which seems to posses all the required ingredients for CR programs. There is a strong tradition of excellent and varied basic research in the public sector. That sector is known for its capabilities and success and is a strong and reliable foundation for the required basic research for CR.

The Industry has also emerged as a strong participant in the R&D projects, due to legal actions and liberalization in the early 1990s, and the evolvement of the world economy and knowledge-based economy since then. In recent years, more and more R&D projects have been transferred to India in recognition of the capabilities of the country.

Government recognition and support—from policy to departments responsible for different aspects, as well as, executive organizations intended to support the growth of the economy based on Science and Technology—is evident and have been evolving since 1947. The downside of that government awareness is the relatively large portion of the national R&D investment, which is government-based, compared to the private sector.

While all the ingredients are present, the task itself is huge considering the size of the country, the diversity of the technologies, and the general size of the sectors involved. The future actions that can be recommended are mainly two:

1. The development of regional CR programs.
2. The development of institutional Technology Transfer units in the Academy.

However, the formation of regional (state size) CR programs tailored along similar lines, but adapted to the specific needs of the relevant state and its infrastructure, in both research organization and Industry, can help promote the general goals.

A cautious development of institute-based commercialization units, that would help bring together the Industry and Academy (public research sector), improve the cooperation and exchange between them, and increase the rate of Technology Transfer, is recommended. This development, while potentially expansive will increase the diversity of applied technologies tested by the Industry, as per their marketing viability and relevance. As a side benefit, these units and the increased exchange will also help India attract additional international R&D centers.

Bibliography

Ahuja, G. (2000). The duality of collaboration: Inducements and opportunities in the formation of inter-firm linkages. *Strategic Management Journal*, 21(3), 317–343.

Audretsch, D.B., and Feldman, M.P. (1996). R&D Spillovers and the Geography of Innovation and Production. *The American Economic Review*, 86(3), 630–640.

Barr, P.S., Stimpert, J.L., and Huff, A.S. (1992). Cognitive change, strategic action and organizational renewal. *Strategic Management Journal*, 13(special issue), 15–36.

Brooks, H. and Randazzese, L.P. (1998). University-Industry relations: The next four years and beyond. In L.M. Branscomb, F. Kodama and R. Florida (Eds), *Industrializing technology: University-Industry linkages in Japan and the United States* (pp. 361–400). Cambridge, MA: The MIT Press.

Brown, S.L. and Eisenhardt, K.M. (1998). *Competing on the edge*. Boston Massachusetts, USA: Harvard Business School Press.

Cabral, L.M.B. (2000). R&D cooperation and product market competition. *International Journal of Industrial Organization*, 18 (7), 1033–1047.

CBS. (2003). *Business Research and Development 2000–2001*. Jerusalem, Israel: CBS.

Cool, K., Dierickx, I., & Jemison, D. (1989). Business strategy, market structure and risk-return relationships: A structural approach. *Strategic Management Journal*, 10(6), 507–522.

D'Aspremont, C. and Jacquemin, A. (1988). Cooperative and non-cooperative R&D in duopoly with spillover. *The American Economic Review*, 78(5), 1133–1137.

Doz, Y.L., Olk, P.M., and Ring, P.S. (2000). Formation processes of R&D consortia: Which path to take? Where does it lead? *Strategic Management Journal*, 21(3), 239–266.

Doz, Y.L. (1996). The evolution of cooperation in strategic alliances: Initial conditions or learning processes? *Strategic Management Journal*, 17(special issue), 55–83.

Dyer, J.H., and Nobeoka, K. (2000). Creating and managing a high performance knowledge-sharing network: The Toyota case. *Strategic Management Journal*, 21(3), 345–367.

Department of Science and Technology (DST) (2009a). http://www.dst.gov.in/stsysindia/about-sys.htm (information downloaded on October 5, 2009).

Department of Science and Technology. (2009b). http://www.dst.gov.in/about_us/ar07-08/chem-scie.htm#rd (information downloaded on October 5, 2009).

Department of Science and Technology. (2009c). http://www.dst.gov.in/stsysindia/industrial-research.htm (information downloaded on October 5, 2009).

Etzkowitz, H. (1999). Bridging the gap: The evolution of Industry-University Links in the United States. In L.M., Branscomb, F. Kodama, and R. Florida (Eds), *Industrializing technology: University-Industry linkages in Japan and the United States* (pp. 203–233). Cambridge, MA: The MIT Press.

Etzkowitz, H., and Leydersdorrf, Z. (1997). *Universities in the global knowledge economy: The triple helix University-Industry-Government relations.* London, UK: Cassell Academic.

EU. (2003). *Communication from the Commission; Investing in research: an action plan for Europe.* COM (2003) 226 final. Available online at: http://ec.europa.eu/invest-in-research/pdf/226/en.pdf

EU. (2006). *Encourage the reform of public research centers and universities, in particular to promote transfer of knowledge to society and industry.* Final report of the CREST expert group, March.

Fontana, R., Geuna, A., and Matt, M. (2006). Factors affecting university–industry R&D projects: The importance of searching, screening and signaling. *Research Policy, 35*(2), 309–323.

Friedman, T.L. (2006). *The world is flat–a brief history of the globalized world in the twenty-first century* (Hebrew edition). Tel Aviv, Israel: Aryeh Nir Publishers.

Grant, R.M. (1997). *Contemporary Strategy Analysis.* Malden MA: Blackwell Publishers.

Gulati, R. (1995). Does familiarity breed trust? The implications of repeated ties for contractual choice in alliances. *Academy of Management Journal, 38*(1), 85–112.

IMEC website (2008). www.imec.be/ Information downloaded on October 2007.

Kaiser, U. (2002a). An empirical test of models explaining research expenditures and research cooperation: Evidence for the German service sector. *International Journal of Industrial Organization, 20*(6), 747–774.

Kaiser, U. (2002b). Measuring knowledge spillovers in manufacturing and services: An empirical assessment of alternative approaches. *Research Policy, 31*(1), 125–144.

Kamien, M.I., and Zang, I. (2000). Meet me halfway: Research joint ventures and absorptive capacity. *International Journal of Industrial Organization, 18*(7), 995–1012.

Kamien, M.I., Muller, E., and Zang, I. (1992). Research joint ventures and R&D cartels. The *American Economic Review, 82*(5), 1293–1306.

Katsoulacos, Y., and Ulph, D. (1998). Endogenous spillovers and the performance of research joint ventures. *The Journal of Industrial Economics*, XLVI (3), 333–357.

Katz, M. (1986). An analysis of cooperative research and development. *Rand Journal of Economics*, 17(4), 527–543.

Krishna, V.V. (2009) ERAWATCH research inventory report: INDIA. Downloaded from http://cordis.europa.eu/erawatch/index.cfm?fuseaction=ri.content&topicID=4&countryCode=IN (accessed on October 28, 2009).

Kyvik S., and Olsen, T.B. (2008). Does the aging of tenured academic staff affect the research performance of universities? *Scientometrics* 76(3), 439–455.

Laredo, P. (1998). The networks promoted by the Framework Program and the questions they raise about its formulation and implementation. *Research Policy*, 27(6), 589–598.

Luukkonen, T.(1988). The difficulties in assessing the impact of EU Framework Programmes. *Research Policy*, 27(6), 599–610.

———. (2000). Additionality of EU Framework Programmes. *Research Policy*, 29(6), 711–724.

Magnet (2007) www.magnet.org.il (accessed in 2007).

McKelvey, W. (1997). Quasi-natural organization science. *Organization Science*, 8(4), 352–380.

Miyagiwa, K., and Ohno, Y., (2002), Uncertainty, Spillovers, and Cooperative R&D. *International Journal of Industrial Organization*, 20(6), 855–876.

Mowery, D.C., Nelson, R.R., and Sampat, B. (1999). The effects of the Bayh-Dole Act on U.S. university research and technology transfer. In L. M. Branscomeb, F. Kodma, and R. Florida, (Eds). *Industrializing knowledge: University-Industry linkages in Japan and the United States* (pp. 269–306). Cambridge, MA: The MIT Press.

NSF website (2008). http://www.nsf.gov/statistics/randdef/business.cfm (information derived from the website in 2008).

Olk, P. (1991). *The Formation Process of Research and Development Consortia.* Unpublished doctoral dissertation, University of Pennsylvania, Pittsburg.

Parker, D.D. and Zilberman, D. (1993). University technology Transfers: Impacts on local and US economies. *Contemporary Policy Issues*, 11(2), 87–99.

Parkhe, A. (1993). Strategic alliance structuring: A game theoretic and transactions cost examination of interfirm cooperation. *Academy of Management Journal*, 36(4), 794–829.

Pastor, M., and Sandonis, J. (2002). Research joint ventures vs. cross licensing agreements: An agency approach. *International Journal of Industrial Organization*, 20(2), 215–249.

Porath, A. (2003). Directed evolution in strategy and management sciences. *Foresight*, 5(3), 33–42.

———. (2004). Intellectual property by-laws in national and multinational programs: A comparison of the EU Framework Programs and the Israeli

Magnet Program. *Proceedings of International Conference, EARMA*. Bucharest, Rumania.

———. (2006). Legal incentives to economic growth–the case of the Israeli R&D Law. *Managerial Law*, 48(3), 322–333.

———. (2007). The Structured research joint venture as a new organizational form for R&D. *ISC Conference*. Jerusalem: Israel.

———. (2008a) Preparing country and firms for slow down in the economy—The structured research joint venture (SRJV) option. *Review of International Comparative Management*, 9(5), 68–79.

———. (2008b) Joint Venture Forming mechanisms under structured programs. Working-paper proceedings of PhD workshop at Austauschprozesse: Extracting the value out of University-Industry Interaction. Muenster, Germany.

Ring, P.S. and Van de Ven, A. (1994). Structuring cooperative relationships between organizations. *Strategic Management Journal*, 13(7), 483–498.

Rogers, E.M., Yin, J., and Hoffmann, J. (2000). Assessing the effectiveness of technology transfer offices at the U.S. research universities. *The Journal of the Association of University Technology Managers*, 12, 47–80.

Rosenberg, N. (1990). Why do firms do basic research (with their own money)? *Research Policy*, 19(2), 165–174.

Sanchez, R., and Mahoney, J.T. (1996). Modularity, flexibility, and knowledge management in product and organization design. *Strategic Management Journal*, 17(winter special issue), 63–76.

Siegel, D., Waldman, D., and Link, A. (1999). Assessing the impact of organizational practices on the productivity of university technology transfer offices: An exploratory study. *Working paper 7256, NBET working paper series*. Cambridge, MA: National Bureau of Economic Research.

Slaughter, S. and Leslie, L.L. (1997). *Academic Capitalism: Politics, Policies and the Entrepreneurial University*. Baltimore, USA: Johns Hopkins University Press.

Spender, J.C. (1996). Making knowledge the basis of a dynamic theory of the firm. *Strategic Management Journal*, 17(winter special issue), 45–62.

Stern, I. and Pozner J.E. (2007). Organizational size, performance and frequency-based imitation: A test of competing hypotheses. Working Paper, ISC.

ST Policy. (2003). downloaded from http://www.dst.gov.in/stsysindia/stp2003.htm#c15. Accessed on October 5, 2009.

Tao, Z., and Wu, C. (1997). On the organization of cooperative research and development: Theory and evidence. Opening remarks. *International Journal of Industrial Organization*, 15(5), 573–596.

Teece, D.J. (1996). Firm organization, industrial structure, and technological innovation. *Journal of Economic Behavior & Organization*, 31(2), 193–224.

Thursby, M., Thursby. J., and Mukherjee, S. (2005). Are there real effects of licensing on Academic Research? A life cycle view. Working paper 11497 (available online at: http://www.nber.org/papers/w11497).

Uzzi, B. (1997). Social structure and competition in interfirm networks: The paradox of embeddedness. *Administrative Science Quarterly*, 42(1), 35–67.
Van Geenhuizen, M. (1997). Universities and knowledge-based Economic Growth: The case of Delft (NL). *Geo Journal*, 41(4), 369–377.
Vonortas, N. (2002). Inter-firm cooperation with imperfectly appropriable research. *International Journal of Industrial Organization*, 12(3), 413–435.
Yun, K.L., Park, Y.S., and Ahn, B.H. (2000). Spillover, competition and better R&D organization. *The Japanese Economic Review*, 51(3), 448–461.

About the Author

Amiram Porath is currently a private consultant for Business Development in Israel, which includes working on national and regional projects. He has previously worked at the Tel Aviv University, Israel, as an International Relations Officer from 2000–2008 and as a faculty member with Derby University from 1998 to 2000. He had a PhD from the Tel Aviv University—Recanati School of Management in Business Strategy Focusing on Industry–Academy Cooperation.

He served as a national expert on the CREST, advising expert group focused on how to "promote the reform of public research centers and universities," in particular to promote transfer of knowledge to society and industry. He also served as an external policy expert to the High Level Expert Group on Reporting of Intellectual Capital for Increased Investment in Research and Development.

His areas of special interest are Business Development and Strategy formulation for High-Technology Firms, Licensing, Technology Transfer, and Strategic Cooperation.

He is also a reviewer of *International Journal of Social Economics* (IJSE) and has been honored by the Italian Republic with a knighthood [CAVALIERE (OSSI)] in 2008.